THE TAROT CHEAT FORMULA

DISCOVER YOUR DESTINY IN THREE EASY STEPS

CLAIRE STONE

Published in the United Kingdom by:
Scorpio & Pisces Press

Text © Claire Stone, 2024
Images bought from Mira MagickCharms
Cover Design by Louise Androlia
Formatting by The Amethyst Angel

The moral rights of the author have been asserted.

All rights reserved. No part of this book can be reproduced by any mechanical, photographic, or electronic process, in the form of a phonographic recording; nor can it be stored in a retrieval system, transmitted, or otherwise be copied for public or private use, other than for 'fair use' as brief quotations embodied in articles and reviews, without prior written permission of the author.

Disclaimer:

The information given in this book should not be treated as a substitute for professional medical advice; always consult a medical practitioner. Any use of information in this book is at the readers discretion and risk. Neither the author nor the publisher can be held responsible for any loss, claim or damage arising out of use, misuse, of the suggestions made, the failure to take medical advice or for any material on third party websites.

A catalogue record for this book is available from the British Library.

ISBN: 978-1-7385070-0-9

*In loving memory of Kancho Ted Devlin.
The most beautiful man I have ever been blessed to know.
May you bathe in the light of the Divine.
Until we meet again.
Sensei Rei.*

PRAISE FOR THE BOOK

Claire is like a breath of fresh air. So incredibly gifted and her knowledge of the tarot is absolutely second to none.
~ Chris Riley, Award winning Celebrity Psychic & Author of *You must be Psychic.*

I knew nothing about tarot before reading this book. Thanks to Claire I've now got a great understanding of the deep wisdom of tarot, and not just the surface information.
~ Richard Lister, Author of *The Book of Runic Astrology.*

This is the book I wish I had when I picked up my first deck of tarot cards! In the Tarot Cheat Formula Claire breaks each of the 78 cards of the tarot down and explains what they can mean in each area of your life so that you can go from absolute tarot newbie to reading for yourself in minutes. If you want to get started reading the tarot for yourself FAST, then you absolutely need this book! As a seasoned tarot pro, I've also found this book has given me new insights and meanings to draw on in my own readings for myself and in readings for clients.
~ Victoria Maxwell, Author of *Witch Please.*

Claire is amazing and her book is a great tool and resource that the world of Tarot truly needs! I love the way it is structured and easily guides the reader through the basics of working with the Tarot. This book is a must-have for anyone who feels called to work with the Tarot, and maybe for those that already have but need more structured guidance on how to practically use the Tarot in an easy and fun way! Claire is an amazing intuitive and expert on the Tarot, and with so many years of experience and her connection to the divine realms of the angels, this book provides such a wealth of knowledge and wisdom. Thank you, Claire!
~ Shereen Oberg - Author of *The Law of Positivism.*

CONTENTS

ABOUT THIS BOOK	1
HOW THE THREE-STEP FORMULA WORKS	3
THE MAGICK'S IN THE QUESTION	4
SPREADS	5
PSYCHIC HYGIENE	7
CONCLUDING THE READING	8
SHUFFLING TIPS	8
GENERAL SPREAD	9
WORK SPREAD	12
LOVE SPREAD	15
FINANCIAL SPREAD	18
SPIRITUALITY SPREAD	21
WELL-BEING SPREAD	24
EXTRA CHEATS	26
THE ELEMENTS MINOR ARCANA CHEAT	26
PUTTING IT ALL TOGETHER	27
THE ELEMENTS IN SPREADS	27
THE PERSONALITY CHEAT	28
EXERCISE 1 – THE FOOL'S JOURNEY	29
EXERCISE 2 – COURT CARD DOPPELGÄNGERS	29
EXERCISE 3 – COURT CARDS WHO'S WHO	30
NUMEROLOGY CHEAT	30

CARD MEANINGS: THE MAJOR ARCANA — 33

0 THE FOOL	34
01 THE MAGICIAN	37
02 THE HIGH PRIESTESS	40
03 THE EMPRESS	43
04 THE EMPEROR	46
05 THE HIEROPHANT	49
06 THE LOVERS	52
07 THE CHARIOT	55
08 STRENGTH	58
09 THE HERMIT	61
10 THE WHEEL OF FORTUNE	64
11 JUSTICE	67
12 THE HANGED MAN	70
13 DEATH	73
14 TEMPERANCE	76
15 THE DEVIL	79
16 THE TOWER	83
17 THE STAR	86
18 THE MOON	89
19 THE SUN	92
20 JUDGEMENT	95
21 THE WORLD	98

CARD MEANINGS: THE MINOR ARCANA — 101

THE SUIT OF WANDS — 102

THE ACE OF WANDS	103
THE TWO OF WANDS	106

THE THREE OF WANDS	109
THE FOUR OF WANDS	112
THE FIVE OF WANDS	115
THE SIX OF WANDS	118
THE SEVEN OF WANDS	121
THE EIGHT OF WANDS	124
THE NINE OF WANDS	127
THE TEN OF WANDS	130
COURT CARDS: THE WANDS ARCHETYPES	**133**
THE PAGE OF WANDS	134
THE KNIGHT OF WANDS	137
THE QUEEN OF WANDS	140
THE KING OF WANDS	143
THE SUIT OF CUPS	**146**
THE ACE OF CUPS	147
THE TWO OF CUPS	150
THE THREE OF CUPS	153
THE FOUR OF CUPS	156
THE FIVE OF CUPS	159
THE SIX OF CUPS	162
THE SEVEN OF CUPS	165
THE EIGHT OF CUPS	168
THE NINE OF CUPS	171
THE TEN OF CUPS	174
COURT CARDS: THE CUPS ARCHETYPES	**177**
THE PAGE OF CUPS	178
THE KNIGHT OF CUPS	181

THE QUEEN OF CUPS	184
THE KING OF CUPS	187

THE SUIT OF SWORDS — 190

THE ACE OF SWORDS	191
THE TWO OF SWORDS	194
THE THREE OF SWORDS	197
THE FOUR OF SWORDS	200
THE FIVE OF SWORDS	203
THE SIX OF SWORDS	206
THE SEVEN OF SWORDS	209
THE EIGHT OF SWORDS	212
THE NINE OF SWORDS	215
THE TEN OF SWORDS	218

COURT CARDS: THE SWORDS ARCHETYPES — 221

THE PAGE OF SWORDS	222
THE KNIGHT OF SWORDS	225
THE QUEEN OF SWORDS	228
THE KING OF SWORDS	231

THE SUIT OF PENTACLES — 234

THE ACE OF PENTACLES	235
THE TWO OF PENTACLES	238
THE THREE OF PENTACLES	241
THE FOUR OF PENTACLES	244
THE FIVE OF PENTACLES	247
THE SIX OF PENTACLES	250
THE SEVEN OF PENTACLES	253
THE EIGHT OF PENTACLES	256

THE NINE OF PENTACLES	259
THE TEN OF PENTACLES	262

COURT CARDS: THE PENTACLES ARCHETYPES — 265

THE PAGE OF PENTACLES	266
THE KNIGHT OF PENTACLES	269
THE QUEEN OF PENTACLES	272
THE KING OF PENTACLES	275
ALSO BY CLAIRE STONE	278
ABOUT THE AUTHOR	279

ABOUT THIS BOOK

As a lifelong student of Tarot, I have noticed how people's attitude towards the psychic world has changed over the years. No longer is it a tool only to be used by "the seventh son of the seventh son," travellers, witches, and born psychics. At last, Tarot has become readily accepted by the modern world and can be embraced by anybody who takes a fancy to it. That's why I am offering something different with this book—a fresh approach that makes Tarot even more accessible and easy to understand. These days, there is less interest in who invented the Tarot or the Tarot basics that are frequently covered in most books and courses. Let's be honest. When it comes to Tarot, are you ever going to read the whole book in one go? Or, like me, would you flick through the pages to investigate the specific card you have just drawn? Life's busy enough, so I have created this revolutionary system so you can consult the cards without any prior knowledge of cartomancy (psychic card reading).

You have probably noticed how versatile Tarot meanings can be. This is what people tend to find most challenging: determining how the cards connect to a particular area of concern. You could spend hours researching online or rifling through books only to discover a vague overall card meaning, or even worse, find so much information that you become overwhelmed having to sift through what does and doesn't fit your question. Let me give you an example: The Four of Pentacles is a good card to pull in association to finances, but if your enquiry is related to romance, then that's an entirely different story. What does a money card mean in terms of love?

You see, cartomancy is not a case of one card fits all. Your interpretation can and will change depending on your question, card position, and surrounding cards. It may sound like there is a lot to consider, and there is, but you can relax—I've got you covered.

With this book, you can easily locate the meaning of your cards in a range of common life situations, making the process exceptionally straightforward. It really couldn't be any easier.

With my foolproof method, you don't need to know anything about Tarot to perform a reading. Once you get to grips with my super easy three-step formula, you will be confidently shuffling away with no more than this book and your deck of cards. You can start right now if you want to. You don't even need to read the whole book because I've taken the pain out of having to memorise cards and thinking about asking the "right" question. You can dive right into the "How the Tarot Cheat Formula Works" section, and off you pop. You can say goodbye to those perplexing moments when you find yourself puzzled by card interpretations, wondering, "What does it mean?"

You can use any Tarot cards that you own to go with this book, but if you have not yet made a purchase, I highly recommend the Universal Rider-Waite deck. Most Tarot books are based on this deck, so it would be a good investment.

If you want to learn about the basics, such as history, symbology, psychic development, spirit guides, and all the practical sides of Tarot, keep your eye out for my next book and check out my online courses.

Next, I will explain how the unbelievably easy three-step cheat formula works.

HOW THE THREE-STEP FORMULA WORKS

In this book, I've provided the comprehensive meaning for all seventy-eight cards in the Tarot deck. Furthermore, I have devised six categories for each card based on the most common questions asked to psychic readers. The cheat process keeps things simple and will save you so much time. The categories include what your Tarot card pull means in:

- General
- Work
- Love
- Finances
- Spirituality
- Well-being

Here are the three steps:

1. Choose which of the six categories listed above best suits the nature of your reading. If none of the themes seem to fit, choose a general reading.

2. Locate the specific spread for your area of enquiry, laying the cards out as directed.

3. Using the contents page, locate your chosen cards (one by one) to discover what messages the cards have in store for you!

Remember, you only need to read the section that relates to the category of your enquiry. You may wish to use the keywords for extra support, as they apply to all types of readings.

For example, let's say your reading will be themed around a romantic relationship. In that case, you would choose the love spread. Once you have dealt the cards as directed, you are all set to discover the significance of those cards. If the first card was the Magician, you would locate the Magician card meaning and read the section titled "Love reading." It's as easy as one, two, three.

It's important to note that the whole meaning will not apply to you word-for-word. That would be an impossible feat. Take what fits and leave out what doesn't. The keywords and additional cards in the spread will help you build a clearer picture of what the cards are trying to convey. Also, think about the artwork. If the card was a photograph, what stories might the photographer have captured? You will find more cool cheats later in the book.

The six categories themselves are self-explanatory. However, if you need a few pointers when choosing your spread, I have added some context about questions and card layouts in the next chapter to help you decide.

THE MAGICK'S IN THE QUESTION

When it comes to Tarot reading, you have three choices.

1. Choose a specific spread which is themed to the nature of your enquiry.

2. Go all out with a general spread and see what wants to be revealed.

3. Make up your own questions.

Using a spread is a good idea if you have a specific topic with several questions. Tarot often works like this: If you don't ask, you don't get. I see this all the time in my practice. A client will arrive and not reveal a single word. They want you to answer their question without asking it. Most of the time, the reason for their visit will be crystal clear, yet occasionally, the cards will not mention the very reason they seek guidance. Why? If readings are too "general," you may receive the answers the cards think you need to hear the most. For example, the querent (the person having the reading) wants to know all about a new business idea, yet they have been ignoring a pressing marriage issue. The cards know that without addressing the relationship first, there will be no means of running a successful business, so they will bring to light whatever needs immediate attention.

This is why general and specific questions are great. Just remember to have a question or intention in mind. It could be as simple as shuffling while thinking, "What do I need to know?" With spreads, the questions are already asked for you, but feel free to tweak them to suit your reading.

SPREADS

A spread is a structured arrangement that an oracle or Tarot reader uses to lay out their selected cards. Performing a Tarot spread is incredibly easy. The layouts are numbered, indicating where each card should go, and each position also comes with a designated meaning or question. Spreads give your reading a clear pathway to follow and help you deliver your reading with a sense of purpose and clarity.

There are six spreads in this book to choose from. As aforementioned, if none of the categories seem to fit your question, then choose the general spread. Here is a brief overview of the spreads.

GENERAL READING SPREAD

A general reading offers insight into a person's life overall. This type of reading is often selected when someone doesn't have specific questions in mind. They might just want to know what the future has in store. The spread I use for general readings is called the Celtic Cross. This is probably the most popular Tarot spread that exists.

WORK READING SPREAD

A work reading is performed when someone has questions regarding their career. They may be wondering if a new job lies on the horizon, perhaps a promotion, or whether they should stick to their job at all. This spread will uncover any challenges someone might be facing at work and provide guidance on how they may achieve their work goals.

LOVE READING SPREAD

A love reading delves into the status of a relationship of any kind, including friendships and romance. People have love readings to discover how others truly feel about them and to determine whether things will work out well. This reading is designed to bring any relationship concerns to the forefront, offering guidance on addressing issues effectively to maintain or establish harmony.

FINANCIAL READING SPREAD

This reading is different from the career reading. Not everyone has a career, but everybody is affected by the state of their finances. Furthermore, money isn't solely gained from working. It can be inherited, invested, gifted, and so on. Someone may choose this reading when they want to know if an investment would be worthwhile or if more financial support is on its way. It can also provide information on how the querent may improve their finances.

SPIRITUALITY READING SPREAD

This type of reading is focussed solely on the querent and connects to the core of their soul. There are times in life when people feel lost or disconnected because they have been ignoring their true desires. This reading will offer deep wisdom from the inner voice within. It also reveals messages from spiritual guides.

WELL-BEING READING SPREAD

By law, a psychic cannot diagnose or discuss matters of health. However, the state of one's well-being can be addressed with this reading. This is a good spread to perform for yourself, as we commonly put our own needs on the back burner. Gain inspiration and get your mind, body, and soul back on track with the guidance from this spread.

You are welcome to use any other spreads you find online or create for yourself. The Tarot card meanings in this book will pair well with any spreads or questions.

Before you get shuffling, I would like to share a few tips with you so that you get the most out of your Tarot card readings.

PSYCHIC HYGIENE

Before you perform your spread, I highly recommend you take a few minutes to familiarise yourself with activating psychic protection and cleansing your energy. When your energy is clear your readings will be more accurate and you will be protected from picking up psychic debris, which will wear you down over time.

First, set the intention to cleanse your energy and make yourself a clear channel. You can do this by lighting incense or burning dried herbs, passing the smoke through your cards and around your aura (energy field surrounding your body). In Britain, our ancestors called this Saining (Scottish) and used herbs such as juniper, lavender, rosemary and mugwort. There are many ways to clear your energy without herbs or smoke. You could use sound therapy or other methods if you prefer.

Once you have cleansed your energy, you call in (invite) the energy of the Divine to guide and protect you. This is a very personal choice—some people like to call in ascended masters, deities, or ancestors. I like to call in the angels. Choose what resonates best with your traditions.

Here is a prayer that I use to invoke Archangel Michael. While saying it, I imagine the blue light of St Michaels' cloak descending upon me, shrouding me in the light.

> *"Archangel Michael, Archangel Michael, Archangel Michael,*
> *Under your wings I stand*
> *Protected by Divine command*
> *In every direction shield me*
> *In your light and love please seal me*
> *So be it."*

Next, you would perform your spread, but if you're reading this for the first time, then carry on until you have fully digested the next topic, concluding the reading. It's important that you can close the reading effectively.

CONCLUDING THE READING

If your reading was for somebody else, cleanse your cards and your aura once again, just as you did at the start. This will disconnect your energy from the querent and ensure you remove psychic debris that doesn't belong to you. People can release a lot of emotions during a reading.

The final step is to psychically close down:

1. Give thanks to the spiritual beings who assisted you during the reading.

2. Your third eye chakra can naturally awaken when you are using your intuition, even if you didn't intentionally open it. Imagine closing the psychic energy centre located on the forehead as though you were closing an inner eye.

3. Earth your energy by having a drink and walking about barefoot.

Now you have learned the basics of safely reading Tarot cards, you're ready to begin!

Here are a few words on shuffling.

SHUFFLING TIPS

Shuffle the cards with a question in your mind or simply ask, "What do I need to know?" When you feel the urge to stop, lay out the cards one by one, as shown in the diagram of the spread. I like to continue shuffling between choosing each card. However, you may prefer to cut the deck into three stacks and take all cards from the top of the pile you feel most drawn to. Have a play around and see which feels best for you.

GENERAL SPREAD

THE CELTIC CROSS

This spread was first published in Arthur Waite's (co-creator of the Rider-Waite-Smith deck) 1910 book, The Pictorial Key to the Tarot. Waite refers to this spread as "an ancient Celtic method of divination."

This is probably the most well-known Tarot spread. Traditionally, this layout uses ten cards. However, I have always used twelve for a little more context. There may be several variations online. This spread is wonderful for a general reading as it sheds a little light on many aspects of the querents life. Here's how to use it.

Remember to protect your energy before you use the Celtic Cross spread for a general reading. When you feel centred, shuffle the cards, laying them out as shown in the image below.

When you have selected all twelve cards, combine the question allocated to each position below with the general sections of the cards you have drawn.

Card 1 – The Present

Sometimes called the 'heart of the matter', this card represents your present circumstances and the energy surrounding you. This position reveals the focus of the reading.

Card 2 – What Crosses You

This card is seen as a bridge connecting the three cards of past (5), present (1), and near future (6). "What crosses you" can represent hurdles (or people) that prevent you from shifting smoothly towards your desired goal.

Card 3 – What's Above You

Also known as the 'crowning card', the "what's above you" position represents what is on your mind. What ideas, worries or thoughts have been consuming you?

Card 4 – What's Below You

This card represents the foundation of the reading. It may reveal a deeply rooted belief or a past action that created the framework for today's situation. This card may also help you to identify repeating patterns that hold you back.

Card 5 – The Past

Everybody has a past, but what is revealed here is relevant in terms of the journey between the past, present, and future cards. See "the past" as what has happened recently that has contributed to who you are today.

Card 6 – The Near Future

This card represents what is going to happen next. Remember, this is not the outcome of the entire reading. See it as the next notable phase before the story is concluded with the last three cards. This card usually manifests pretty quickly, sometimes within days.

Card 7 – Your Personality

This card reveals your personality traits or how you feel about yourself. It's ok if you don't have a court card here! If you drew Death, for example, it could mean you are feeling exposed or are ready to end an old way of being. The Two of Swords could indicate you are indecisive. The Empress might suggest you are feeling broody or motherly, and so on.

Card 8 – The Environment

This card describes your environment at work or home. If you find someone overbearing, such as a moody relative or a bully boss, they may appear in this section. It depends on how much impact they have on you.

Card 9 – Hopes and Fears

Positive cards reflect your ambitions, and negative cards can indicate where you feel the grips of fear.

Cards 10, 11, and 12 – The Outcome

These three cards sum up the outcome of the reading, as in what will occur in the future. As a rule of thumb, these cards usually manifest within twelve months. However, I tend to find the cards playing out much earlier.

Once you have read the general card meanings, remember to psychically close the reading as described earlier in "Concluding the Reading."

> **TIP:**
> Bookmark the page of your chosen spread so you can easily find it while flipping back and forth between the card meanings. Alternatively, write the card positions and your chosen cards in your journal. This way, you also have a record of your reading to look back on.

WORK SPREAD

Use this card spread to discover all that you need to know about your work life. Remember to prepare yourself energetically before you take part.

When you are ready, shuffle the cards while thinking about your work situation or simply think of the word "work." Intuitively select your cards, laying them out one by one, as shown in the diagram. When you have dealt your cards, pair up the question posed in the positions with the work section of your card pulls.

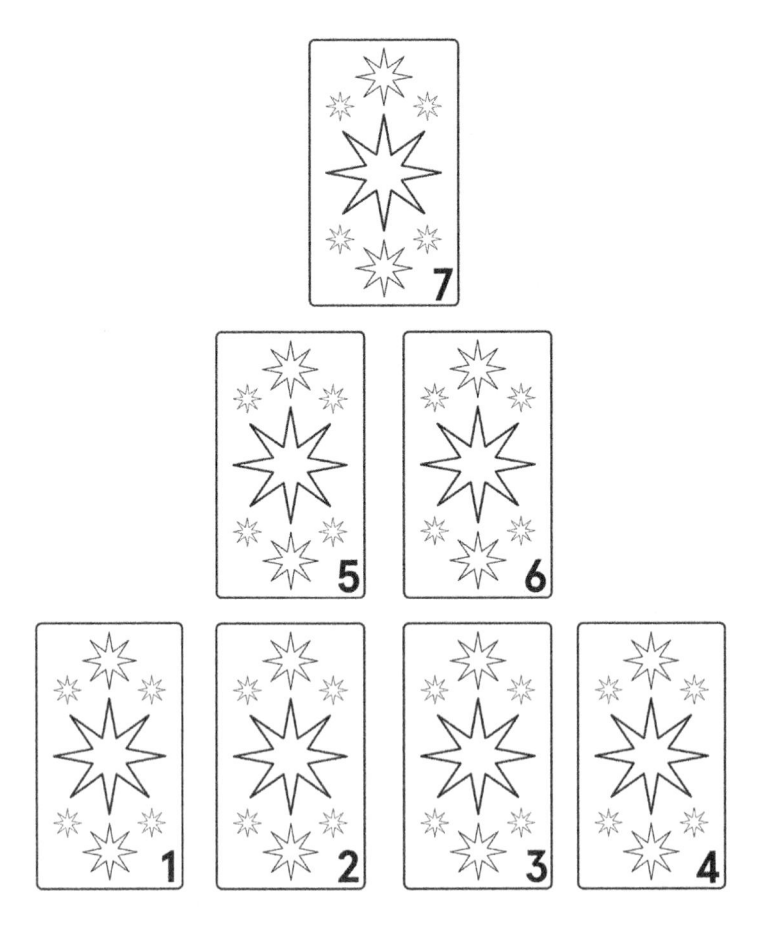

Card 1 – The Current Situation

This card will reveal how you feel in terms of your career.

Card 2 – The Shadow

This card reveals if anything is going on behind the scenes that you are unaware of. This can range from a subconscious belief preventing you from attaining your goals to a person throwing a spanner in the works or simply a case of the wrong timing. Whatever the issue, this card will unearth who or what is blocking your progress.

Card 3 – Goals

This card describes your dreams and ambitions.

Card 4 – Advised Action

This card advises how to proceed to ensure the best chances of happiness and success. Follow this guidance to achieve your goals.

Card 5 – Future Prospects

This positioning offers insight into how your career will progress in the future. It could herald a new job or reveal stepping up the career ladder or retirement—or perhaps you are contented with things remaining the same.

Card 6 – Destiny

This card will provide insight into what kind of work fulfils your soul. You may need to take your time with this one as it may provoke some deep thinking or even surprise you. Look at all the imagery and use the keywords.

Card 7 – Outcome

This card reveals the outcome of your career enquiry.

Once you have read the work interpretations of your selected cards, be sure to psychically close the reading as described earlier in "Concluding the Reading".

TIP:
Whether you choose to shuffle for others or let them handle the cards is a matter of personal preference. I tend to shuffle and ask the querent to tell me when to stop. That way, they are choosing their own cards without imprinting their energy upon them. If you are selecting the cards for the querent, make sure that you set the intention in your mind that you are choosing for them. If someone wants me to pick their cards, I will say their name in my mind to ensure I am drawing cards for them and not myself. Some people are not confident in choosing their own cards.

LOVE SPREAD

This spread uses fifteen cards. I like to use more cards when it comes to relationships because we know how complex they can be. Such an important topic deserves a decent number of questions.

Remember to call in psychic protection as directed earlier before you lay out the cards as shown in the diagram. You will find all your answers in the love section of your chosen cards.

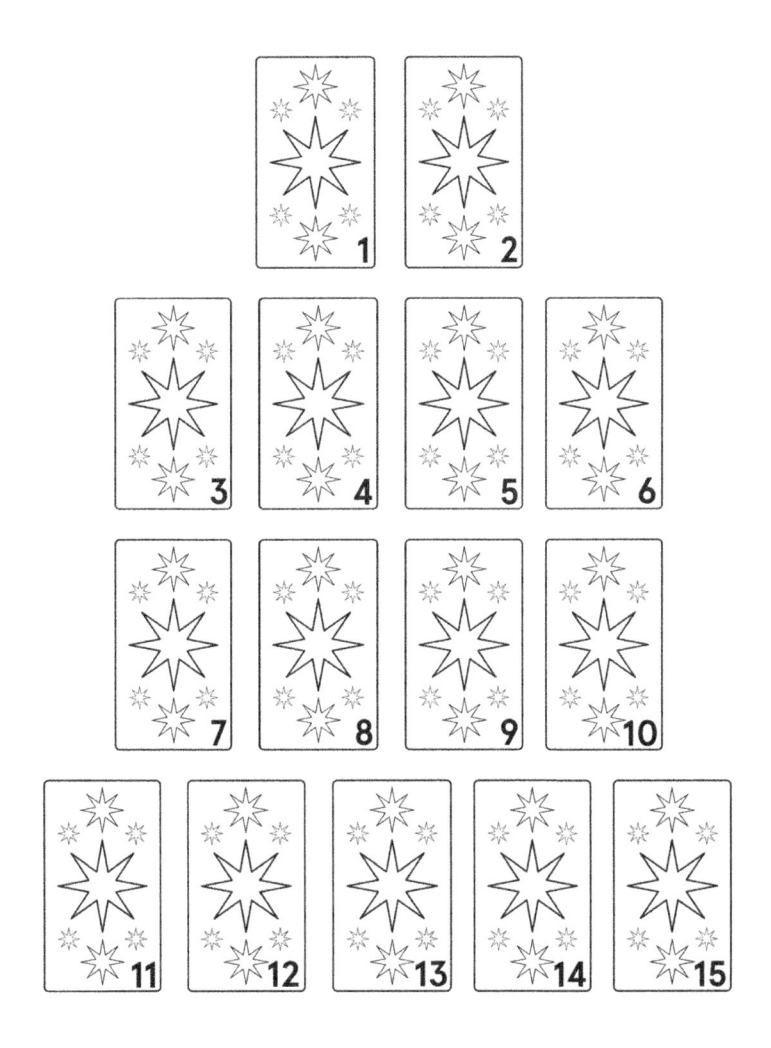

Card 1 – How the Relationship Started

This card describes the relationship at the beginning.

Card 2 – The Status of the Relationship Today

This card position reveals the current status of the relationship.

Card 3 – How the Person Sees You

Discover how you are seen/thought of by the other person.

Card 4 – How They Truly Feel About You

Discover the true feelings of your person in mind.

Card 5 – Their Fears or Reservations

Find out what fears or reservations the other person may have about this relationship.

Card 6 – Where They Hope This Relationship Will Go

This card will reveal if the person in question has pure motives and if they are truly invested in this relationship. This is what they really want.

Card 7 – How You See This Person

This card describes how you perceive the other person.

Card 8 – How You Truly Feel About Them

This card identifies how you truly feel about the person in question.

Card 9 – Your Fears and Reservations

This card will reveal any conscious or subconscious fears or concerns that you have about the relationship.

Card 10 – Where You Hope This Relationship Will Go

This card describes how you hope to see this relationship progress.

Card 11 – External Influences to Bear in Mind

This card can represent other people, circumstances, or beliefs that are impacting the relationship. You may be aware or unaware of these influences.

Card 12 – The Strengths of the Relationship

These are the positive qualities that support the relationship. This is what you have going for you.

Card 13 – The Weaknesses of the Relationship

This card uncovers any weak spots that may be hindering this relationship.

Card 14 – Advice

This card offers the most positive action steps to consider, ensuring the best outcome of the relationship.

Card 15 – The Future of the Relationship

Based on how things are going (sometimes you can improve the outcome by implementing positive change), this is the outcome of the relationship.

Once you have discovered the meaning of your cards in the love sections, complete the reading by psychically closing your energy down, as described earlier in "Concluding the Reading."

> **TIP:**
> If you are unhappy with the answers your reading has provided, rather than sit in fear, be proactive. Your future is not always set in stone. Ask the cards, "Can I do anything to change this outcome?" A positive card will mean yes, and a negative card will mean no. If the answer is yes, shuffle again and ask, "What can I do to prevent or change this pathway?" You are the co-creator of your destiny.

FINANCIAL SPREAD

This spread will help you assess your financial health and discover how to improve your revenue.

Remember to call in psychic protection as directed earlier and lay out the cards as shown in the diagram below. You will find all your answers in the finances section of your chosen cards.

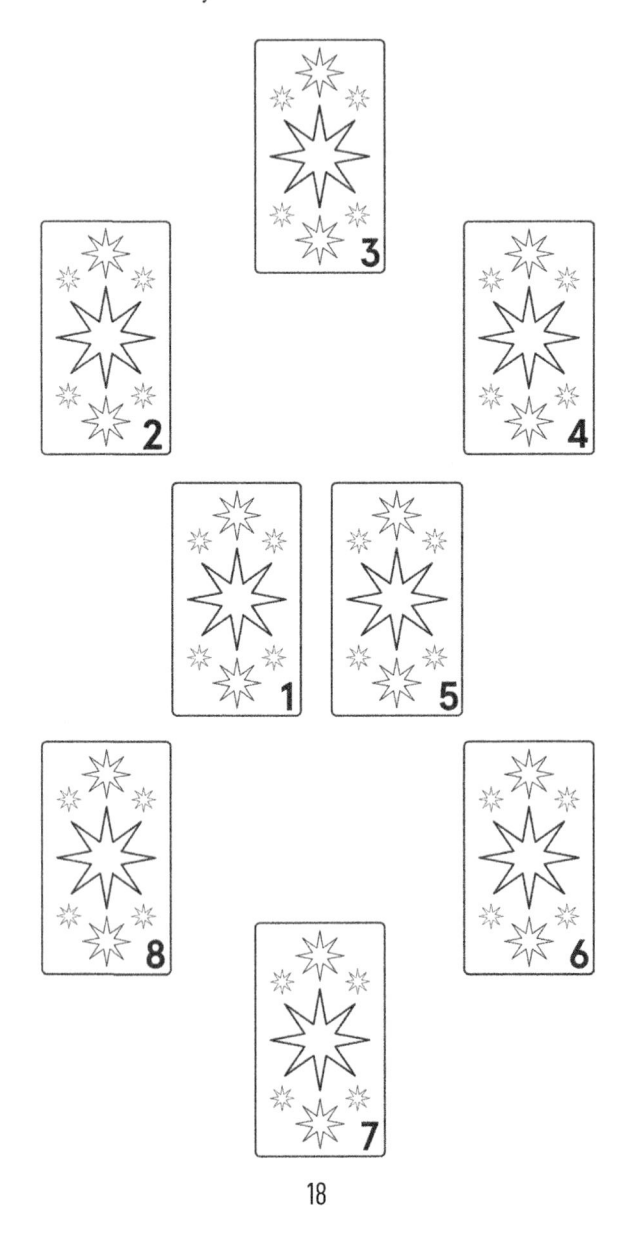

Card 1 – Your Current State of Finances

This card describes your financial status—are you wealthy, struggling, curious about an investment, etc.?

Card 2 – Wealth Belief System

Your beliefs about money are important because they can help or hinder your manifestations. This card identifies your true beliefs about wealth.

Card 3 – What You Are Subconsciously Manifesting

This card identifies the effects of your beliefs on your financial health. Remember, you can rewire your subconscious mind with hypnosis and affirmations if needed.

Card 4 – What You Can Do Today to Manifest the Wealth You Deserve

This card will reveal action steps to take to improve your finances. It could suggest gaining insight, taking risks, further education, etc.

Card 5 – Investments

This card will describe any investments that you may be thinking of. If this isn't applicable, use this card as a compass that points you in the direction of where you can best invest your time or money.

Card 6 – Will Your Investments Bear Fruit

This card will let you know if the investment analysed in the previous card will reap financial rewards. If you don't have an investment in mind, this card will show you if your finances are about to improve.

Card 7 – How to Think to Manifest Wealth

This card reveals how you need to think to attain your desired financial success.

Card 8 – The Outcome

This card reveals how your finances will look over the next six months.

When you have read the interpretations of your reading, remember to psychically close your energy as described earlier in "Concluding the Reading."

> **TIP:**
> You can always add your own questions to a reading if there are specific answers that you are looking for. For example, you could ask, "Is this the best person to invest in my new business idea?" Or, "Will this venture be successful? Will I see a return on my money?" And so forth.

SPIRITUALITY SPREAD

This spread will help you tap into your soul's wisdom and connect you with your team of spiritual supporters. This is a perfect spread to use if you are on the journey of self-discovery or are feeling stuck on your current path. Divine guidance is always available to you; this layout will help you to retrieve it. You can change the words from "spirit guide" to "guardian angel" if you prefer.

Invoke psychic protection before you lay out the cards, as shown in the image. You will find all your answers in the spirituality section of your chosen cards.

Card 1 – Your Spirit Guide

This card represents the personality of your main spirit guide. You will gain extra clarity by observing the person/archetype on the card. Are they male or female? Do they seem strict (swords)? Or maybe they are healers (cups). Are they young (at heart) or old (and wise)? Take some time to look at the symbols on the card and read up on the meaning.

Card 2 – Your Higher Self

This card represents the essence of your soul. The higher self is the wise, all-knowing aspect of you that is free from the limitations of the ego. See this as the purest version of yourself.

Card 3 – Spiritual Lesson

This card reveals a spiritual teaching or lesson that is important for you to focus on now, e.g. forgiveness, manifesting, self-love, etc. Reviewing the lesson and implementing change can help you progress spiritually.

Card 4 – Good Karma

This card describes some good luck that's on its way to you. This is a blessing that you have earned by past actions of kindness.

Card 5 – Ego

Discover how the ego (lower self) is holding you hostage from rising into your true power.

Card 6 – What Your Spirit Guide Wants You to Know

This card reveals a direct message from your spirit guide.

Card 7 – What Your Higher Self Wants You to Know

This card reveals a message from the highest aspect of your soul.

When you have read the interpretations of your reading in the spirituality sections, remember to psychically close your energy as described earlier under "Concluding the Reading."

TIP:
When you perform a reading, be mindful that you are asking the cards questions. The questions are revealed in each position of the card spread. You could ask that question in your mind when shuffling if you want to.

WELL-BEING SPREAD

This spread will shed light on the status of your well-being and suggest improvements to help restore the balance in your mind, body, and soul. Remember, this reading is not a substitute for medical advice, and by law, you cannot divulge medical opinions to the querent. This is a lovely spread for yourself.

Ensure that you call in psychic protection before you lay out the cards, as shown in the diagram. You will find all your answers in the well-being section of your chosen cards.

Card 1 – Mind

This position describes how you are feeling mentally.

Card 2 – Body

This card delivers insight into the condition of your physical body.

Card 3 – Soul

This card describes the health of your psychic energy and the form of your soul.

Card 4 – What to Look Out For

This card gives you the heads up on which aspect of your well-being needs your immediate attention.

Card 5 – Action Steps

This card explores possible action steps that could restore optimum well-being.

When you have read the interpretations of your reading in the well-being section, remember to psychically close your energy as described earlier in "Concluding the Reading."

> **TIP:**
> Don't take the card meanings in this book word-for-word. Choose what fits and cast aside what doesn't apply.

EXTRA CHEATS

The Tarot cheat formula provides enough insight to give yourself and others a reading without researching the meaning of the cards. However, if your love of Tarot grows and you would like to dive a little deeper, then keep on reading to discover a few more cheats. I have created the following techniques so you can learn as quickly and effortlessly as possible.

THE ELEMENTS MINOR ARCANA CHEAT

The four suits of the Minor Arcana are divided into the four elements of creation. They are earth (pentacles), air (swords), fire (wands), and water (cups). Each element has its own dynamics with different qualities, strengths, and challenges.

By having a brief understanding of the elements, you can pick up the meaning of the cards without knowing too much about them at all.

Here are the elements and their keywords:

EARTH (PENTACLES)

Keywords: Material world, money, stability, work, education, practicality, planning, abundance, the physical body, down-to-earth, homelife, progress.

Associations: Pentacles are associated with the element of earth, symbolising the tangible and material dynamics of life. This suit represents the physical world, including finances, work, and the practical aspects of living. Think of stability and abundance when interpreting pentacles cards.

AIR (SWORDS)

Keywords: Thoughts, intellect, communication, conflict, clarity, truth, life passages, logic, challenges, harshness, mental health.

Associations: Swords correspond to the element of air, representing mental processes and communication. This suit deals with the power of thoughts, clarity of the mind, and the sometimes sharp edge of conflict. Think of intellect and communication when you draw the swords cards.

FIRE (WANDS)

Keywords: Passion, energy, action, career, creativity, inspiration, motivation, willpower, confidence, warmth, lust, sex.

Associations: The wands suit represents the element of fire, which is dynamic and transformative. It signifies the spark of passion and the driving force behind your actions. Think of what motivates you when the wands cards arise.

WATER (CUPS)

Keywords: Emotions, relationships, intuition, love, feelings, connections, healing, feelings, spirituality, family and loved ones.

Associations: Cups are linked to the element of water, which symbolises love and the emotions. This suit reflects matters of the heart, including love, friendships, and the deep well of intuition within. Think of feelings and connections when interpreting cups cards.

PUTTING IT ALL TOGETHER

When you have mastered the keywords of each element, pair those associations with your imagination! The Rider-Waite Tarot deck is symbolic, the artwork on each card playing out one of life's many scenarios.

Let's try this together now. Take one card from the Minor Arcana. What powerful story could you conjure if you had to tell a tale based on the picture you see? How does the image make you feel? What could the characters be thinking or doing in the image? Make notes about your observations.

Now, infuse your ideas with the keywords allocated to the element of your card. This is like adding a splash of colour to bring your story to life. Can you see how much easier card interpretation has just become? Have fun making up stories as you work your way through the deck.

THE ELEMENTS IN SPREADS

The next time you perform a reading, I want you to notice the elements in your card spread as a whole. For example, if the majority of the cards are cups, you would know that love, family, and happiness are high up on the priority list of the person having a reading. On the contrary, if there are many swords present, it could indicate that this person may be lonely, lacking in loving relationships, or wrapped up in their own world. Think about which suits/elements are in excess and which are lacking in each spread.

I love this hack. I wish I had known it sooner, as it gives you an instant thread of energy to start reading from. The next cheat that I am about to share came about quite naturally. You might already do this yourself.

THE PERSONALITY CHEAT

This cheat requires some initial effort and takes time to build upon, but it will save you so much time in the future. The following exercises aim to get you fully acquainted with the characters in the deck. Allow me to explain.

Eventually, you will likely associate a certain character in the deck with someone you know. For instance, my husband is the King of Pentacles through and through. So, when a client appears as the King of Pentacles in their reading, I can describe their personality to an absolute tee. No psychometry or astrology, just absolute knowledge of the King of Pentacles archetype (personality). This ability blows people away. Here are some exercises to help you understand the archetypes of the deck so that when your clients draw those cards, you will already know a lot about the person they represent.

EXERCISE 1 – THE FOOL'S JOURNEY

The Major Arcana already has its own story attached to it. This story was coined The Fool's Journey by Eden Gray. It is a metaphor for the journey of one's life. The Fool is the soul who embarks upon this adventure. On his way, he encounters the twenty-one archetypes of the Major Arcana, learning their wisdom teachings and experiencing the many facets of life. The Fool's Journey does have some striking similarities to Joseph Campbell's Hero's Journey.

TRY THIS
When you have some time for yourself, grab your journal and a snuggly blanket and head to my website to experience the Fool's Journey with my free bonus meditation. Make notes afterwards. The link is as follows: www.clairestone.co.uk/thefool.

EXERCISE 2 – COURT CARD DOPPELGÄNGERS

When you can, carve out some time to explore the court cards. Focus on one suit at a time so that it's digestible. Notice if the personality traits of the page, knight, queen, and king of your chosen suit remind you of anyone in particular. It doesn't have to be a family member. The Queen of Swords could be similar to your boss or an old schoolteacher. You could even use fictional characters that you know from books or a TV series. Be totally creative with this and make notes. When these cards arise in your reading, be confident and describe the personality of the card in great detail. Think of the court cards as being a doppelgänger of the person being read.

Eventually, you can do this with the entire deck. As I said, this takes effort, but imagine how amazing your readings will be! This is a good investment of time if you plan on reading professionally.

EXERCISE 3 – COURT CARDS WHO'S WHO

Take all the queens out of the deck and notice their differences. Who in the deck do you think they would bond well with? Who might they not get on with? Who is the most confident queen? Who seems most caring? What are the strengths and weaknesses of each of the queens? Who would make a good consort for each queen and why? If you were giving a reading to the queens, which cards would they like to receive? What would light them up inside?

Later, try this exercise with the pages, knights, and kings.

NUMEROLOGY CHEAT

You can enhance your ability to quickly interpret your Tarot reading by having a basic understanding of numerology. Here are some starting points that you can apply to get you going.

The number **one** signifies new beginnings, individuality, leadership, and creation. It's associated with the ace cards in each suit, indicating the inception of a new journey or a fresh start.

The number **two** represents duality, balance, cooperation, and choice. It reflects the idea of partnership, relationships, and the need to make decisions.

The number **three** symbolises creativity, growth, expansion, and self-expression. It's often associated with the manifestation of ideas and the development of a concept.

The number **four** represents stability, structure, security, and foundation. It's a number that suggests the need for order and a solid base to build upon.

The number **five** signifies change, challenges, adaptability, and conflict. It represents a period of transition and adjustment.

The number **six** is associated with harmony, balance, love, and relationships. It reflects cooperation and an emphasis on matters of the heart.

The number **seven** represents analysis, introspection, spirituality, and wisdom. It's related to self-reflection and connecting to the Divine.

The number **eight** signifies power, abundance, success, and manifestation. It's related to material and financial matters and the realisation of goals.

The number **nine** symbolises tying up loose ends and the stage just before completion. This can be a powerful and enjoyable but often demanding time where a final slog is required to reach the finish line. It represents the culmination of a cycle and a broader understanding of life's lessons.

The number **ten** represents achievements, unexpected endings, recovery, and the end of a cycle. It often signifies forced change and the rewards that come after hard work.

Now you have an element, an image/story, and a number vibration to apply to the Minor Arcana cards.

The Major Arcana also has elements and associated numbers. You will discover those meanings on each of the cards coming up next.

CARD MEANINGS: THE MAJOR ARCANA

0 THE FOOL

The Fool represents a person who is up for an adventure! They are feeling inspired and ready for change. Even though they may be about to embark upon a new project or journey with some level of risk, they are optimistic and confident enough to take a chance. The card says: Go and explore!

The Fool card is **zero**. He is the beginning, the end, and everything in between.

Element: Air

GENERAL READING

In general situations, the Fool is a very exciting card to receive. It speaks of fresh starts and new adventures. This is a time when you can afford to take calculated risks. You will attain your end goal, even if you can't quite see how. Just believe that you already have everything you need to succeed. This card is a great omen. Even though the path of life is seldom straight, you are being encouraged to explore uncharted waters. Implement new ideas, embark upon project concepts, and have a bash at anything that has recently taken your fancy.

A new perspective offers you the opportunity to refine yourself in every possible way. You are well-protected. Just make sure you don't have your fingers in too many pies—you don't want to spread yourself too thin.

WORK READING

In work circumstances, the Fool brings fresh starts. Maybe a new job is on the horizon, or you have a strong desire for change. Perhaps you have an amazing idea, but a lack of confidence has prevented you from getting started. This card can reflect that you feel underqualified or not quite ready. Despite this, be assured that it's your time to shine!

Don't compare yourself to others or keep waiting for perfection. Otherwise, you may never get started. Grab opportunities with both hands.

Don't take it to heart if someone has misjudged your abilities. Keep your head down and show them what you're made of.

LOVE READING

In love readings, the Fool indicates that romance is not your current priority. Having a new lease on life and getting things in order are more important. You should be feeling confident and pretty carefree. Even if you aren't thinking about love, an exciting whirlwind romance could be in the air. Anything is possible at this time.

If you are in a relationship, then you are being asked to become the Fool. Lighten up and spend time having fun with your other half. This will propel you both into a period of increased joy and happiness.

If you are asking how someone feels about you, then know the person thinks you're charming but is enjoying their freedom and is not likely to settle down. However, they may be willing to take a chance with you.

FINANCIAL READING

From a financial viewpoint, the Fool says to be wise with cash and investments! You could be tempted to overspend, and even though this is a very optimistic card, you still need to be sensible and think carefully about the future.

If you are inquiring specifically about finances, remain assured that you will get the cash injection you need.

SPIRITUALITY READING

Spiritually speaking, the Fool says, "Don't be afraid to break the mould and forge your own spiritual path." You've transcended your circle, so those unwilling to maintain a high vibration are no longer interesting to you. Remain open; a new yet ancient soul family awaits you.

WELL-BEING READING

Well-being related, this is a great time to make positive, lasting changes for your health. Yet, the Fool says that simplicity is key right now. You may feel the urge to rush into a new health regimen, such as a detox or weight-loss plan, but remember that slow and steady wins the race. However, you should be feeling energised and motivated.

ASSOCIATED KEYPHRASES
Optimism
A new beginning
Go for it
A leap of faith
You have all you need to proceed
Travel
Feeling young at heart
A new job

01 THE MAGICIAN

The Magician symbolises a person who has come into their own. This powerful creator knows exactly what they want and is motivated and enthusiastic to execute their goals. This person is in alignment with their desires. It is as if the Universe itself dances to their command.

This card is number **one** in the Major Arcana. This number represents new beginnings, fresh starts, and golden opportunities.

Element: Air

GENERAL READING

In general, the Magician is an excellent card to draw—it is the "law of attraction in action" card within the deck. The possibilities for success are endless. You've got what it takes to bring all your dreams into fruition; you just need to take action!

You have the potential to change anything that you are unhappy with. The power is in your own hands.

WORK READING

In work circumstances, the Magician is a great omen. Are you after a new job? Then apply for it. Do you want a promotion or pay raise? Then make your wishes clear to your boss and the Universe! If you make a plan and take action, you will inevitability manifest your desires. You have a lot to offer to the world. Show up for yourself.

LOVE READING

In love readings, the Magician reminds you that your relationships will only grow so long as you invest in them! The scales of balance could be slightly uneven if you are focussing on other areas of interest right now.

Your vibrant energy makes you incredibly attractive, so don't be surprised if you receive a romantic offer or few. People are taken in by your charm; it's as though you have them enchanted under your spell.

FINANCIAL READING

From a financial viewpoint, the Magician is a brilliant card to draw. Opportunities to manifest abundance are on the horizon. Be proactive and gently guide more wealth into your life. Don't wait for the money to fall onto your lap; plant your own seeds, and fruit will grow when it's your season. Be confident and independent in your decision-making. This is a great time to make investments.

SPIRITUALITY READING

Spiritually speaking, the Magician reminds you that the kingdom of Heaven lies within. You are currently positioned within liminal space. This place, the in-between worlds, is where the union of Heaven and Earth takes place.

Tap into his magick and create your desired reality. Just ensure your thoughts are pure and for the benefit of all. Don't let these newfound superpowers go to your head. Be humble.

WELL-BEING READING

Well-being related, the Magician indicates that you have the power to increase good health. If you have recently been under the weather, look at your daily regime. Assess your well-being. It could be that some simple tweaks to your diet or implementing some expert tips could make a big difference and get you back on top form. The Magician will give you all the motivation you require. Expect to feel better. You can do it.

ASSOCIATED KEYPHRASES

Successful manifestation
Go for it
Use control
Concentrated energy
Your dreams are coming true
The ability to make magick
An initiation
New beginnings

02 THE HIGH PRIESTESS

This card represents a woman in her power or an aspect of your feminine, intuitive side. The High Priestess is the mystic of the deck. She knows the mysteries of the Universe, yet with her ego tamed, she has no desire to reveal her secrets to the world. She sees the deeper meaning of all things.

Her number, **two**, represents opposites. Our job is to find the centre of duality.

Element: Water

GENERAL READING

In general, the appearance of the High Priestess indicates that you are coming into your spiritual power. This is a very important time for you, and it would serve you well to go within. Your soul is longing for deeper connections. You know that there is more to the mundane aspects of daily life. The great mystery is calling you. Nothing will satisfy your spiritual itch. You must embark upon a journey into the unknown. You are ready to rediscover your true identity, and your psychic gifts are awakening.

WORK READING

In work circumstances, the High Priestess' appearance denotes a time when you may prefer to work alone. Others may seek you out to draw upon your expertise and wisdom, but overall, you feel more efficient when working solo.

Perhaps you feel you are in the wrong career and would be better suited to something spiritual, holistic or something with a more creative flair. You have the ability to see beyond the surface, use this to your advantage.

LOVE READING

In love readings, the High Priestess indicates that you may benefit from having your own space right now. When you are truly contented within yourself, you will naturally attract a suitable lover towards you. You may, however, be quite happy on your own and not need others to fill your cup.

If you are asking how someone sees you, the High Priestess can indicate that you come across as quite the mystery. You are hard to figure out.

FINANCIAL READING

From a financial viewpoint, the High Priestess guides you to trust your intuition when investing your cash. Money-making ideas could be plentiful, but you can gain deeper clarity by contemplating and journaling ideas. You are reminded, however, to keep your cards close to your chest. Other people do not need to know your next step. In fact, their opinions or influence could prove unhelpful.

SPIRITUALITY READING

Spiritually speaking, the High Priestess indicates that you are in a spiritual awakening. You may find yourself interested in crystals, healing, or other esoteric topics. One way or another, your higher self will find ways for you to explore the ancient wisdom rising within you. Your intuition is strong, and you have a compelling desire to connect with a higher power, so what's stopping you?

Your angels and guides are supporting you. Have you noticed them trying to get your attention? Look out for repetitive numbers, white feathers, and increased synchronicities. These are signs you are on the right path.

Keep a journal of your dreams to record important insights as your psychic abilities grow.

WELL-BEING READING

Well-being related, the High Priestess reminds you that nobody knows you better than you know yourself. You already understand how to relax, what foods to eat, and how to take great care of yourself. Now is the time to ensure you are applying your health-boosting wisdom to feel like the vibrant soul you wish to be.

As a natural healer and empath, it would serve you well to be mindful of absorbing other people's energies. Carry a protective gemstone such as black tourmaline to shield yourself and take a shower after being in the company draining people.

If you are transitioning through one of the sacred feminine rites of passage, look for ways to celebrate and honour this process. These rites include first menstruation, pregnancy, perimenopause, and moon pause (if applicable). This can be a wonderful time of self-discovery and personal progression.

ASSOCIATED KEYPHRASES
Trust your instincts
Tapping into Divine knowledge
A wise woman
You are a healer
Protect your idea
Stop and contemplate before taking the next step
A time to pause, non-action
Emotional stability

03 THE EMPRESS

This card represents a salt-of-the-Earth mother figure—a caring woman who has given it her all. Now, she can sit back and admire the fruits of her labour that are beginning to blossom all around her. Contented with how things are, she doesn't beg, chase, or cling to her abundance, for she has mastered the art of giving and receiving. This awareness allows the Universe to provide for all her needs and more.

The Empress is card number **three**. This number represents conception, two blended energies that birth new life.

Element: Earth

GENERAL READING

In general, the Empress signifies the good times. You are about to receive wonderful news or manifest something you have been wanting. Your hard work has paid off; now is your time to savour the rewards. It seems that Lady Luck is on your side. Your dreams are coming true, with plans turning out even better than expected. Your cup is overflowing with love and gratitude.

This is the pregnancy card. Look out for the Ace of Cups or the Three of Cups in the reading to reinforce this conclusion.

WORK READING

In work circumstances, the Empress signifies that you are the go-to for advice. You have a plethora of creative ideas and love to inspire and uplift others. Colleagues feel supported by you. You are well-liked, wise, and easy to talk to.

If you run your own business, things should start to look very rosy. Results are now coming to fruition. You can put your feet up for five minutes and enjoy your creations.

If you are awaiting news regarding work, then expect to hear a positive result.

This card can represent a woman on maternity leave or a stay-at-home parent.

LOVE READING

In love readings, the Empress signifies that love is all around you. Your radiant inner beauty shines brightly, and people cannot resist your warmth and kindness. Some may see you as the woman who has it all and, sadly, may be quite envious of your life. Don't take it personally, though. Remember that you are adored by those who truly matter: your nearest and dearest.

Romantic relationships are the real deal. If you have had any doubt at all, this card assures you that your person thinks the absolute world of you. No one else comes close to you.

If you are looking for love, then you won't be on the shelf for much longer. Stay focused on loving yourself first; before you know it, someone will notice how wonderful you are.

FINANCIAL READING

From a financial viewpoint, the Empress ushers in a time of luxury and abundance. You have the Midas touch. Everything that you nurture with your love and attention is increasing. Your attitude of gratitude keeps the flow of abundance incoming. You are generous and don't grip on too tight. These are the perfect conditions for successful manifestation.

SPIRITUALITY READING

Spiritually speaking, the Empress signifies a time when you feel spiritually connected. You understand your role in the great web of life and your purpose: to create.

You may have developed an interest in the Divine Feminine wisdom teachings. Set the intention to join a women's circle. This is a time of sisterhood.

A WELL-BEING READING

Well-being related, the Empress brings you the gifts of happiness, good health, and vitality. If you are trying for a baby, this card assures you that a pregnancy is in the cards.

Everything that you need and want is within reach. Keep on counting your lucky stars to stay in flow with the Universe.

If you have been working too hard, use this as a notion to take more time to rest and refuel. Meditation, clean foods, and a good pamper will have you glowing in no time.

ASSOCIATED KEYPHRASES
Abundance
Fertility
Nurturing others or a need to be nurtured
A pregnancy
Love
Beauty
A love of life
You are blossoming

04 THE EMPEROR

The Emperor is the most powerful masculine force in the deck. Consort to the Empress, he naturally assumes the role of the father figure. This card can represent a natural-born leader or someone who maintains order and fairness in his domain. He could be a teacher, boss, parent, or an aspect of yourself that is all for serving the greater good.

The Emperor is the solid number **four**. He has everything covered.

Element: Fire

GENERAL READING

In general, the Emperor speaks of a strong masculine presence in your life or the Divine Masculine energy within yourself. If this card refers to yourself, you are being called to stand in your power. It's time to be assertive and define your boundaries, especially if someone is trying to take advantage of you. Logic must trump the heart if you want to attain your goals.

If this card speaks of another, a man in your life may have brilliant solutions to bring order and justice to your problems. However, he can be quite militant and grumpy, so be prepared to take his advice if you seek it out.

WORK READING

In work circumstances, the Emperor could signify a boss or peer breathing down your neck. This person is quite rigid in their ways and always thinks that they are right. Annoyingly, they usually are, but their directness can trigger feelings of unworthiness or even anger. Realise that criticism is impersonal. Rather, this person has incredibly high standards.

If you are being called to summon the Emperor from within your psyche, the message is to roll up your sleeves and get stuck in. Don't shy away from hard work. You are a born leader and will be well-received should you show the world what you are made of.

LOVE READING

In love readings, the Emperor shows up when you are feeling blocked.

If you are in a relationship, you may feel some level of detachment from your partner as the Emperor hides his emotions well. This card can represent a person who has traditional values. He is loyal and very good at taking care of things practically, but if you want more affection, you will have to make all the moves.

If you are single, it's time to let your guard down and allow love into your life. Perhaps you are being a little too fussy. Remember, no one is perfect.

FINANCIAL READING

From a financial viewpoint, the Emperor is an encouraging card. You are highly qualified in your field, and your attention to detail and organisational skills are second to none. Use them to make long-term plans for future investments.

You may have to step up and take financial responsibility for others.

SPIRITUALITY READING

Spiritually speaking, the Emperor brings in the energy of the Divine Masculine and brotherhood. Perhaps you need to be held at this time. Maybe you have been giving too much and must learn to say no. Look within to discover why you may be allowing others to disrespect your boundaries.

Call in the protection of the Divine Father or the archangels to guard you while you rest. Invoke the light of the sun to strengthen and energise you. Masculine protection and wisdom are just what you need at this time.

WELL-BEING READING

Well-being related, the Emperor is a great card to pull! You are feeling revved up and are raring to go. This is an ideal time to start a new exercise plan or eliminate bad habits. Your strong willpower and motivation will see you through.

If you have health concerns, this card reminds you to seek professional advice and not sweep things under the carpet, no matter how small.

ASSOCIATED KEYPHRASES

A great leader
A father figure
Putting your house in order
Having positive boundaries
Fairness
Wisdom
Using logic
Stability

05 THE HIEROPHANT

Consort to the High Priestess, the Hierophant is another spiritual teacher of the deck, but whereas she is solitary and her teachings are internal, the Hierophant has gathered a crowd and teaches in groups or institutions. He represents wisdom in action, a wise person, a teacher, or someone with valuable knowledge to assist others. You need to identify whether you are the teacher or the student within your current circumstance.

The Hierophant card is number **five**. It represents the integration of the elements, just like the five-pointed star. His spirit is the fifth element.

Element: Earth

GENERAL READING

In general, the Hierophant represents coming together in community. His appearance in your spread can indicate that society, the government, schools, religion, or any other type of organisation is affecting your life.

However, you can improve your situation by forming alliances.

Current situations may test your beliefs and bring ingrained subconscious patterns to the surface. You may be questioning everything. Who are you? How have you been indoctrinated? Stand firm in your convictions, but also seek expert advice.

WORK READING

In work circumstances, the Hierophant indicates that teamwork is the key to success. You are open-minded and eager to learn. Your curiosity will lead you onto new pathways. Education may be required to cement your future, so ensure that you embark upon any training courses that will help you to advance.

Don't be afraid to ask for help if you are struggling. People around you will prove to be great allies and be happy to help you out.

LOVE READING

In love readings, the Hierophant can indicate a marriage or a deepening of commitment. This is the card of tradition, so if you are asking where a relationship is heading, receiving the Hierophant is a very good omen because it symbolises planning for the future.

Contrary, if you are wondering why a person won't commit, this card indicates their family could be the reason why. Responsibilities or higher priorities may be getting in the way.

FINANCIAL READING

From a financial viewpoint, the Hierophant reminds you to make wise decisions and seek professional advice from the relevant people. If you are thinking of going into a joint project, then go for it—this card assures you that the partnership will be successful. Financial security can be yours if you play by the rules.

SPIRITUALITY READING

Spiritually speaking, the Hierophant comes to you as your guru. He may manifest as a spirit guide, guardian angel, yoga instructor, or anyone willing to awaken your inner teacher. Remember to show reverence and respect for this person but be mindful not to put them on a pedestal. Ultimately, you walk through the portal; the teacher merely guides you along the way.

If your soul craves companionship, find a psychic circle or spiritual retreat. Being in the presence of like-minded souls will bring you a sense of renewal and purpose.

WELL-BEING READING

Well-being related, the Hierophant suggests that you explore traditional measures. If you have a cold, take vitamins, sleep, and keep warm. Look towards old remedies to improve your health and heal your bodily ailments. Ensure that you also seek out professional advice and be open to taking a new approach to wellness. Let the experts help you.

Emotional contentment comes when you are surrounded by family and friends.

ASSOCIATED KEYPHRASES
A spiritual teacher
An expert mentor
Seek professional advice
Becoming part of an organisation
Stick to the beaten path
Marriage
Making a commitment
Learning from the best

06 THE LOVERS

The Lovers represents a person whose mind is focussed on relationships and authenticity. They may be experiencing a range of beautiful yet frustrating feelings of lust, attraction or love. In contrary, it could be that this person is yet to notice that someone is swooning over them

The number **six** within this card relates to union and harmony.

Element: Air

GENERAL READING

In general, the Lovers card usually appears when you are feeling loved up or have a romantic enquiry. You feel alive with passion and your heart is awakening. Maybe you are intoxicated with an idea or person you think will complete you and make you feel whole. There are often choices to be made when this card arises. Just don't allow rose-tinted glasses to taint your view of reality.

WORK READING

In work circumstances, the Lovers is a great omen. It shows that you understand others and their motivations. Relationships are harmonious, and there is a sense of appreciation among the workforce.

This is a time of expansion, and if the opportunity to move up the career ladder arises, this will be a difficult choice for you to make. Let your heart decide.

LOVE READING

In love readings, the Lovers is a fabulous card to draw. It indicates that there have been positive developments within your relationships. This can be a deepening of an existing relationship, a time when you feel especially connected and appreciative of your partner.

The Lovers also shows up when our head has been turned and we feel a strong desire and sexual attraction towards another. If you are asking how someone feels about you, then this card reveals that you are perceived in an erotic way. If you are asking where a relationship will lead (if anywhere), a sexual liaison or even marriage could take place! But don't get too carried away just yet and be sure not to abandon your needs by getting swept up in a whirlwind of lust.

This card can also indicate a time of reconciliation and forgiveness.

FINANCIAL READING

From a financial viewpoint, the Lovers indicates that you can easily get carried away. You may need to watch your spending as you feel frivolous and generous. This is a positive card but also one of overindulgence, so have fun but in moderation.

SPIRITUALITY READING

Spiritually speaking, the Lovers card indicates that you are creating more harmony within your mindset. You have undergone shadow work and began to face your inner demons, resulting in a deep connection to the Divine and a newfound love of life. From this higher perspective, you admire the beauty in all things.

WELL-BEING READING

Well-being related, the Lovers indicates that you are feeling quite happy right now. Previous health issues melt away, and well-being is restored. Give yourself a pat on the back because positive lifestyle choices have ushered in this time of healing. Keep up with your self-care regimes. This is a true act of self-love.

ASSOCIATED KEYPHRASES

Feeling loved up
Lust
Meeting a new romantic partner
A return to health
Temptation
Weighing up your options
Letting go of the apron strings
Passion

07 THE CHARIOT

The Chariot represents a person who is on a mission! He has a clear vision of what he wants and is on his way to successfully executing his goals. The proverbial wheels are in motion, and nothing can stop him now.

In this card, the number **seven** denotes bringing in all aspects of yourself.

Element: Water

GENERAL READING

In general, the Chariot moves you forward with great speed and confidence. This card is all about taking action. If you have not yet begun, it's time to ask yourself what it is you're waiting for.

Taking one step at a time is absolutely fine. Just make sure that you get going. You will pick up momentum and confidence as you go along.

WORK READING

In work circumstances, the Chariot is a brilliant card to pull. It indicates that you are perceived as an incredibly competent individual. You have the ability to draw people together and create brilliant strategies that inspire all components to work in harmony. Your strengths are many, but you are especially admired for your discipline and self-confidence.

Persevere with projects or self-employment, you are coming into your own. Your lucky stars are lined up. With good fortune, energy, and motivation, failure is not an option.

LOVE READING

In love readings, the Chariot can wheel you in several directions. Look for surrounding cards for clarity. On one hand, it can signify doubts creeping in. You may find yourself wondering if this person is really for you. You may be tempted to look elsewhere for contentment. But this is usually a blip because the sphinxes in the card are bound by destiny. Put in the extra effort, and your relationship will be back on course.

If a lover has strayed and this card emerges, chances are they will be back.

Sometimes this card can indicate a holiday romance or meeting someone while on your travels. This relationship will progress quickly. There is a feeling of familiarity with this person; it is like you have known them in a past life.

FINANCIAL READING

From a financial viewpoint, the Chariot can easily manifest all the abundance he needs and wants. This brilliant card ushers in a time of prosperity. If you need to make investments, make a clear plan of how you can stretch your resources to get you across the finish line and reach your goal. Be confident, you can do it.

SPIRITUALITY READING

Spiritually speaking, the Chariot invites you to delve deeper into the great mystery. You are ascending forward in leaps and bounds and may experience newly awakened psychic gifts, astral projection, or lucid dreams.

Learn about your Merkabah, your chariot of light, but be sure to keep yourself well grounded. You are enthusiastic and want to understand everything now but remember to keep everything in balance.

WELL-BEING READING

Well-being related, the Chariot card indicates that you are feeling great. Your plans are coming together, bringing you a deep sense of satisfaction. You are in high spirits—you feel optimistic, and life is looking good. Tackle any niggling health issues head-on, and all will be well.

A short period of seclusion can re-energise you. Take a day off and spend time in your own company.

ASSOCIATED KEYPHRASES
Moving forward
Travel
Taking action
Willpower
Determination
Making progress
Victory
Momentum

08 STRENGTH

The maiden in the Strength card serves as a reminder that you do not need to use brute force or physical strength to win over adversaries and foes. This card represents a person who is undergoing challenges and needs to tap into their feminine strengths to overcome complications. Acting with compassion and having control over your emotions is key to successfully navigating through challenges at this time.

In this card, the number **eight** represents her success. She has controlled her primal fears of the root chakra and allowed the flow of kundalini to rise through her crown.

Element: Fire

GENERAL READING

In general, the Strength card makes an appearance when your endurance is being put to the test. Situations around you are challenging, but the Universe will never throw at you more than you can handle. You are stronger than you think.

There is a blessing in the burden if you can rise above the snares of the ego.

WORK READING

In work circumstances, the Strength card denotes overwhelm. Are you getting flustered? Do you feel you have bitten off more than you can chew? Are people pressuring you with tasks and deadlines?

Take a breath. Know that you have got this. Try and make things as simple as possible. Get organised; if you are struggling, be honest and ask for help. Being vulnerable will ensure you receive the support you need.

If you are seeking employment, you may feel as though you are at your wit's end looking for suitable work. Hang on in there. Remember, not all doors are meant for you. Keep knocking, and the right one will surely open.

LOVE READING

In love readings, the Strength card appears when you or a lover are going through a period in which one of you may need handling with kid gloves. Perhaps you are exiting a rocky patch. If so, compassion and gentle consideration of each other's needs are called for. You may need to dig deep within yourself but be patient; this is a time for re-addressing balance and deep healing.

If you are single, you are being reminded to work on loving yourself first. You may have a lot on your mind right now, making this the most important time to implement some TLC.

If you are asking for the outcome of a relationship, this card says you can get through anything if you take the right approach. If you handle it correctly, this blip will bring you and your partner closer together in the long run.

FINANCIAL READING

From a financial viewpoint, the Strength card calls you to grab the bull by the horns.

Don't run away from financial issues. Rake through your bills, work out your income, and outgoings. Plan how you can bring harmony to your bank balance. See where you can cut back. When you put your mind to it, you can accomplish anything.

If investments or business have been slow, persevere and think about how you can expand. Can you add another string to your bow to give you that extra edge?

SPIRITUALITY READING

Spiritually speaking, the Strength card reminds you to embrace your feminine side. Go with the flow and let your heart lead the way forward.

You may feel overly sensitive to the struggles of others. If so, regularly practice clearing your space and strengthening your energy with toning or protective crystals.

WELL-BEING READING

Well-being related, the Strength card asks you to treat yourself as lovingly as you treat others. Up your self-care. Have self-respect, and don't allow others to cross your boundaries.

You have a deep internal power within you—tap into it for extra motivation. This will increase your willpower and strength, enabling you to withstand any storm.

ASSOCIATED KEYPHRASES
You will get through this
Compassion is the way forward
You can do it
Utilize your feminine powers
It takes great strength
Be brave
Consider others' needs
Courage

09 THE HERMIT

The Hermit can represent your spiritual teacher, a spirit guide, or someone seeking wisdom. The path to enlightenment is a journey that must be undertaken alone, so it's not unusual for this person to be a loner or suffer from loneliness. Yet if he takes time to journey deep within his soul, he will find what he seeks. This is his opportunity to become wisdom embodied.

The number **nine** in this card represents the closing of a cycle.

Element: Earth

GENERAL READING

In general, the Hermit is a deeply spiritual card. His appearance in a spread signifies that you need some time alone to integrate change and process what has occurred within you. On your quest for truth, you have realised that the external world cannot fill your cup. All the answers that you are seeking are within. You, alone, are the only person who can uncover the hidden gems awaiting your discovery.

There is a stirring within your soul. Trust where you are being led.

WORK READING

In work circumstances, the Hermit card reveals that you are very knowledgeable in your subject and are sought out for advice. Keep studying and learning all there is to know. As the eternal teacher/student, you were born to lead the way.

If you find yourself at a crossroads, embark upon a journey of self-discovery. The path will reveal itself along the way.

LOVE READING

In love readings, the Hermit signifies a need for time and space to reflect. You may not be interested in sex or romantic relationships at this time.

If there is uncertainty within your relationship, hold off making big decisions until you can gain more clarity. You may feel lonely or unsupported by your partner. You need to decide whether this relationship is fulfilling your needs and, if not, how you could make things better.

If you are single, you must learn to be happy in your own skin. This part of your journey is meant to be walked alone.

FINANCIAL READING

From a financial viewpoint, the Hermit suggests that you should think long and hard before parting with your cash. There could be some pitfalls that you are currently unaware of. It's better to take your time making financial decisions.

Review the facts and gain perspective. This is not the time to allow others to influence your spending.

SPIRITUALITY READING

Spiritually speaking, the Hermit beckons you to trust your intuition. Your eyes may well deceive you, but energy never lies. Trust your inner knowing, or you will kick yourself later!

This is a very exciting card to pull if you are involved in psychic or spiritual development. It assures you that you are on the right path and stepping up a level. Expect tests of faith to measure your spiritual maturity.

Keeping up with a daily spiritual practice will keep you centred and ensure your soul expansion continues. It's time to align with your inner sage.

WELL-BEING READING

Well-being related, the Hermit says that patience is needed if you are awaiting health-related news. Try to shore up hopeful feelings and remain positive. The answers to your prayers will soon come to light.

A period of rest could do you a world of good, but above all, this card indicates a need to quiet the mind. Take measures to cultivate more peace in your life.

If you are feeling lonely, reach out to old friends. A bit of company will be immensely beneficial.

ASSOCIATED KEYPHRASES
Go within
Find your spiritual calling
Embody the inner guru
Important psychic insights
Psychic gifts awaken
Lucid dreams
A search for inner peace
Accelerated spiritual growth

10 THE WHEEL OF FORTUNE

This card appears when someone is about to experience big changes. It represents adjustments in circumstances, aligning with destiny, and catching up with karma. Everything in the natural world is in a constant state of flux. What comes up must eventually come down, and vice versa. When this great card appears, the hand of fate is about to spin the wheel. There is an alignment with destiny.

The Wheel of Fortune is numbered **ten**. Ten is the number of changes.

Element: Fire

GENERAL READING

In general, the Wheel of Fortune reminds you that nothing remains the same forever. If you have had good luck of late, challenges may lurk ahead. However, this is a wonderful card to pull if you have recently had your fair share of troubles. It brings a welcomed relief from hardship. Your luck is about to change for the better. Good things are now coming your way.

Remember that you need contrasting situations to learn important life lessons such as humility, compassion, and gratitude.

WORK READING

In work circumstances, the Wheel of Fortune brings you exciting news. Positive change is in the air. If you have applied for a position, chances are you will succeed. You are destined for great things and will soon see developments coming to light. All your efforts were worthwhile. Big rewards will soon be yours.

LOVE READING

In love readings, the Wheel of Fortune is a marvellous card to pull. It can suggest that you are about to meet a destined love interest.

If you are already committed, it can confirm that you have found your soul mate. There is a deep sense of familiarity between you as if you know each other from an ancient past.

Romantic relationships can feel very intense and special. As you may have suspected, your meeting was predestined, and you have karmic plans to play out.

FINANCIAL READING

From a financial viewpoint, the Wheel of Fortune can go either way. It can signify financial loss, bad investments, or a massive stroke of good luck. This can manifest as a winning streak or one of those times where you experience minor setbacks, where things go wrong one after the other.

See neighbouring cards for clarification. Understand that there is a season and reason for everything.

SPIRITUALITY READING

Spiritually speaking, the Wheel of Fortune signifies a time when you feel aligned with destiny. You will notice miraculous synchronicities.

Opportunities will seem to manifest as if from thin air.

What you are actually experiencing is your good karma. The universe is showing you the powerful effect you have on your life via your thoughts and actions. You feel truly connected to a higher power.

WELL-BEING READING

Well-being related, the Wheel of Fortune promises that if you have been under the weather, your health is about to have a big turnaround. You are feeling energised. Complaints become a thing of the past. However, this is not an opportunity to let healthful habits slip.

If you have had issues with your hips, knees, legs, or feet then you are urged to think deeply about your true identity and purpose. Your soul is calling you to walk a higher path that will bring you more joy and contentment.

ASSOCIATED KEYPHRASES
This is a karmic cycle
A turn of good luck
Fortune is on your side
In alignment with your destiny
Travel
Change is in the air
Divine Timing
A life-changing event

11 JUSTICE

The Universe is governed by a series of cosmic laws. In the Justice card, you see a person about to witness the results of the spiritual law of cause and effect. Circumstances unfolding around them are direct consequences of their actions. If they act with integrity and fairness, justice will prevail.

This card is numbered **eleven**. Reduced, we have the number two. This can represent the two sides of the coin. In some decks, this card is switched with the Strength card, number eight.

Element: Air

GENERAL READING

In general, the Justice card can be seen as positive or negative, depending upon what you have been up to! It is a very simple card. Do what is right, and you will be met with the same respect in life.

Yet should you cut corners, cheat, or act deceitfully, know that Lady Justice will be rounding you up to repay these past endeavours. It serves you well to respect the law and maintain your integrity.

WORK READING

In work circumstances, the Justice card can indicate that you may be about to sign a new contract. This is good news if you are applying for work or a new position.

You are fair, honest and have strong ethics. You stand up for what is right.

This card can refer directly to career roles: a lawyer, police officer, government official, social worker, head teacher, correctional officer, surgeon, and more. Basically, it indicates anyone who upholds order.

LOVE READING

In love readings, the Justice card indicates that a relationship is stable. This is one of the cards that indicate marriage or moving in together, becoming legally bound.

If many sword cards are present in the reading, this relationship could be stale and unemotional. You would like to see the Lovers, the Ace of Cups, the Two of Cups, the Six of Cups, or the Ten of Cups paired up to show that romance is still present.

This is a favourable card of reconciliation if a marriage is heading for divorce. There may be a positive turnaround.

FINANCIAL READING

From a financial viewpoint, the Justice card suggests there could be an exchange of contracts. You may be renting or buying a new home. You could be signing a contract for a new promotion.

Equally, Justice can indicate that you are about to receive compensation, payback, or inherit a sum of money.

Seek financial advice about how to invest any surplus income.

If you are paying off a loan or debt, or creating a will, rest assured you will feel more at ease with your finances in order.

SPIRITUALITY READING

Spiritually speaking, the Justice card talks about karma. The situation in which you currently find yourself is a direct result of your past actions. If you are having a run of bad luck and cannot fathom what actions have led to your situation, you may benefit from a past life reading.

If situations seem to be lining up nicely, enjoy this time of reaping that which you have sown.

Know that whatever the case, your soul is ready to align with your higher truth. You are evolving beautifully.

WELL-BEING READING

Well-being related, the Justice card asks if you have been investing in your health and wellness. If you have been lazy and eating junk food in excess, you may have to deal with the toll this has taken on your body. Now would be a great time to consider your well-being.

If you are about to undergo surgery, this card assures you that the procedure will go well.

ASSOCIATED KEYPHRASES
Legal matters
The signing of contracts
New home, loans, car lease, etc.
Justice will prevail
Marriage
An encounter with the law
Weighing up your options
Lawyers, police, social services, surgeons,
and people of authority help you

12 THE HANGED MAN

The Hanged Man can represent a frustrated person. This is someone seeking answers, movement, or change, but circumstances or lack of motivation keep them stuck. They may feel as though they are suspended in time. Yet, there is an opportunity to be realised by hanging in limbo. It's as though the Universe has slowed them down on purpose.

In this card, the number **twelve** reduces to three. This again connects to the alchemical three primes of matter: sulphur (the soul), mercury (the spirit) and salt (the body).

Element: Water

GENERAL READING

In general, the Hanged Man brings you to a standstill. You may have encountered a stumbling block in the road and can't seem to navigate your way around it. Or perhaps you have run out of resources and cannot move forward. You are desperately seeking answers or inspiration.

Know that in time, they will come. Try not to give in to feelings of impatience. Instead, take advantage of this slower time.

WORK READING

In work circumstances, the Hanged Man asks you to change your perspective. Things may seem topsy turvy, so don't make any irrational decisions. Bide your time; an epiphany will allow you to see things with new eyes before long.

If you are enquiring about a new job, the Hanged Man says not yet. Fear not; a better-suited opportunity will come along.

LOVE READING

In love readings, the Hanged Man indicates that you may not know where you stand within a relationship. You and your partner are not quite on the same page, leaving you confused. An honest conversation is needed. If you are unsure of your feelings, take some time out to gain perspective. Again, don't make any sudden moves until you are certain you are seeing things clearly.

If you are single and are asking if you will meet someone very soon, the answer is not just yet. Be patient and find other things to focus on.

FINANCIAL READING

From a financial viewpoint, the Hanged Man asks you to slow down and watch your spending. If finances seem slow or are drying out, try not to get caught up in worry and the vibration of lack. Take a sensible approach; don't bury your head in the sand but energetically surrender to your situation.

Let go of attachment and return to the basics of manifestation: a clearly defined goal, taking action, and having a deep sense of gratitude.

SPIRITUALITY READING

Spiritually speaking, the Hanged Man gifts you with an opportunity for spiritual advancement. Your soul desires peace, your spirit craves wisdom, and your heart lusts after the love of the Divine.

Perhaps you need to make some sacrifices to reach new heights. In Latin, the word sacrifice means "to make holy." If your quest is for enlightenment, give yourself away. Let go of your personality and attachments. Meditation will bring the answers you seek.

WELL-BEING READING

Well-being related, the Hanged Man says that your mind is ready for change, but your body needs a rest, or vice versa. Take this time to gather your strength. Relax and replenish your mind. Try gentle exercise to improve your flexibility.

Keep close to Mother Earth to maintain grounded. This card can represent someone with blood pressure issues, poor circulation, or dizziness.

ASSOCIATED KEYPHRASES
Feeling in limbo
A period of waiting
Being patient
Make a sacrifice
Acceptance
A change in perspective
Your world is turned upside down
Looking at something the wrong way

13 DEATH

The Death card represents a person about to endure an ending of sorts. This could mean a job is ending, moving to a new house, or parting ways in a relationship. There is a sense of finality with this card. Whatever comes to close, there will be no going back.

The number **thirteen** on this card represents the completion of a cycle. The ancient Celtic lunar calendar acknowledged thirteen months per year.

Element: Water

GENERAL READING

In general, the Death card foresees you closing the door on a certain area of your life. Sometimes, we are saddened by change, especially if it is unwanted. Remember, in time, another pathway will surely open. This is not the end of the book; it is simply the closing of a chapter. The future is yours to write.

WORK READING

In work circumstances, the Death card indicates a change in your standing. If you were unemployed, then this may be about to change.

If you are asking a work-related question, then big changes may be coming. You could be relocated to a new department or be in for a complete change in the workplace. Perhaps you are about to leave or be laid off.

If you are asking if a job interview will be successful, then on this occasion, it's a no. This is not a time to quit, however. Keep advancing.

LOVE READING

In love readings, the Death card can denote that a relationship will come to an end. At its best, it can indicate a lasting change, but there must be positive clarifying cards to back this up.

FINANCIAL READING

From a financial viewpoint, the Death card asks you to watch your finances closely. Is money slipping through your fingers? This card sometimes appears when you are gambling, wasting money on addictive substances, or spending excessively to feel good. Remember, these highs are temporary and always bring you crashing back down to Earth. Seek help if needed.

SPIRITUALITY READING

Spiritually speaking, the Death card indicates that you are heading into a period of transformation. You may have been subjected to some harsh lessons and are wondering how you will go on.

Try and understand that only false paradigms will be stripped from you as you are primed for the ultimate spiritual test, the death of the Ego.

WELL-BEING READING

Well-being related, the Death card says it's time for a change. What bad habits or negative beliefs are you willing to give up in order to feel better? It's time to reinvent yourself. If you have experienced unexplained weight loss, get yourself booked in for a check-up. This card can sometimes represent bone issues, vitamin deficiencies or malnutrition.

ASSOCIATED KEYPHRASES

Endings
A new beginning is on the horizon
Letting go of an old way of thinking
A breakup
Loss
Impermanence
Transformation
Walking away from something

14 TEMPERANCE

The angel in this card is a skilled alchemist. He represents a person who needs to look at the different aspects of their life to see if they have the winning ingredients to create happiness. Working too hard, drinking too much, or anything else used in excess only leads to anguish. Likewise, deprivation of rest, love, or nourishment eventually leads to resentment and bitterness. By successfully maintaining an overall state of balance, one can attain happiness and the magick of well-being.

In this card, the number **fourteen** reduces to five. This reminds us that anything in excess always results in misery and hardships.

Element: Fire

GENERAL READING

In general, the Temperance card asks you to take appropriate measures to ensure your life is in balance and you take on all things in moderation. Temperance reminds you that the only way to attain true peace is by mixing and combining all areas of your life into one beautiful symphony.

Embody the virtue of patience. This will enable you to maintain a state of contentment while you await the fruits of your labour.

WORK READING

In work circumstances, the Temperance card indicates that you may feel impatient. Remember, there are no shortcuts to the top. Keep showing up and give your best every day. You are constantly improving, and with consistency, you will excel with greatness.

You like to get ahead, and sometimes you think you are faster working alone, but now is the time to let others help you. Hear out other people's ideas. There is value in varying opinions. Take all information into consideration.

LOVE READING

In love readings, the Temperance card may be asking you to put your feet in your lover's shoes. Seeing life from another's perspective can increase your level of understanding. Try not to control others. If you can positively communicate your needs and desires to another, you have the recipe for an incredible union.

If you are single and looking for love, trust that there is someone out there for you. Put yourself out there and show the world the beautiful colours of your personality.

FINANCIAL READING

From a financial viewpoint, the Temperance card has two aspects. This card sometimes arises when a person cannot control their spending and needs guidance to get their finances back on track.

In its positive aspect, this card indicates that investments may be building slower than expected but are growing, nevertheless. Be patient; your seeds are well planted.

SPIRITUALITY READING

Spiritually speaking, the Temperance card invites you to awaken the inner angel within you. Archangel Michael, along with your guardian angel, are drawing particularly close to you at this time.

With a simple prayer you can give them permission to be your advocates. They will help you to learn the wise ways of the angels and discover who you truly are.

WELL-BEING READING

Well-being related, the Temperance card reminds you to consider the components of achieving good health. Anything out of kilt at this time can quickly harm your entire system. Be gentle; don't rush or take on too much. Practice an art that can help you to strengthen your internal energy, such as Aikido, Tai Chi, or Yoga.

Don't be concerned with what others around you are doing. Focus on how their actions are affecting or triggering you. Morihei Ueshiba said, "As soon as you concern yourself with the good or bad of your fellows, you make an opening in your heart for maliciousness to enter."

Sometimes this card can represent someone who has issues with alcohol.

ASSOCIATED KEYPHRASES
Combining
A blending of opposites
Consider others' feelings
A time of healing
Balancing all areas of your life
A guardian angel is protecting you
Alchemy
Share your ideas

15 THE DEVIL

The Devil card appears when someone is feeling irritated, challenged, or uncomfortable. They may be swamped with negativity and cannot seem to get out of their own way. The good news is they get to choose. They can remain enslaved to their problems by listening to the devil on their shoulder, or they can work a little harder on being more positive by listening to the solutions from the angel on their shoulder (reflected in the Lovers card). It's a choice.

This card is numbered **fifteen**. Reduced to six, it connects to the Lovers card. However, unlike the harmony and union we see in the Lovers, the Devil reveals polarised energy and separation.

Element: Earth

GENERAL READING

In general, the Devil card symbolises that which brings you pleasure but also causes pain. It can manifest as an affair or the lover who will never leave his/her wife. It can be the last glass of wine before you quit drinking tomorrow, a day that never comes.

You can no longer mask unresolved pain. Distractions from your truth will only temporarily fulfil you. The cycle of suffering continues until issues are finally addressed.

WORK READING

In work circumstances, the Devil card can represent a workaholic. You are never quite satisfied with yourself and keep pushing to achieve bigger and better. This attitude can get you to the top of the career ladder, but please try and reward yourself a little!

If you are asking how you would feel if you took a new job position, the answer is trapped.

If you are enquiring about a job you recently applied for, this card means you will not be successful; however, see this as a blessing. You have had a lucky escape!

LOVE READING

In love readings, the Devil card has a lustful and sexual undertone, so if you are asking how someone feels about you romantically, then know that the attraction is strong. But remember that this card reflects the animalistic urges of the root chakra, so don't expect too much. Maybe you will get into this person's bed, but not necessarily into their heart.

Toxic behaviours could be causing issues within your relationship. Obsession, trauma-bonding, lust, and giving your power away all come into play with the Devil. Your person has their own demons to face before/if they will fully commit.

Perhaps you feel trapped and cannot see a way out. Gather enough strength to walk away.

If you are single, then perhaps you keep people at arm's length due to being hurt in the past. Know it's safe to be vulnerable and put yourself back out there.

This card can also indicate infidelity. Look out for the Magician, the Three of Cups, the High Priestess, and the Seven of Swords to conclude this interpretation.

FINANCIAL READING

From a financial viewpoint, the Devil card suggests that you may be spending beyond your means. Have a good look at your finances. Be honest with yourself if you are squandering money. The euphoria you feel when making purchases is short-term. You are likely to beat yourself up with guilt and regret if you allow yourself to continue.

If applicable, refrain from lending money to others. You might not get it back.

Thoroughly consider joint ventures. If you have any doubt at all, trust your gut. It could turn out to be more stressful than it's worth.

SPIRITUALITY READING

Spiritually speaking, the Devil card invites you to dive deep into the underworld. You may not feel like your sparkly self but see this uncomfortable time as an opportunity to heal.

Shadow work can help you understand where your emotional triggers took root.

Suppressed trauma will only wreak havoc in your life, so get a therapist to help you work through your past. Remember, diamonds are formed under great pressure. This is an initiation rather than a punishment.

WELL-BEING READING

Well-being related, the Devil card says that you may feel unsupported at this time. As a result of your circumstances, your positive attitude may have slipped. Perhaps you are indulging in food and drink as a form of escapism. It is time to evaluate your habits. If anything does not promote your health and well-being, let it go.

Try not to be too hard on yourself. You can be your own worst critic or a loyal, loving supporter. Actively change your thinking. Learn to see the cup as half full.

ASSOCIATED KEYPHRASES

A need for control or being controlled
Negative thinking
Pessimism
Overindulgent
An affair (see additional cards)
Substance abuse
Addictive behaviour
Feeling trapped in a negative cycle

16 THE TOWER

The Tower card is also known as The Liberator and La Maison Dieu (French, House of God). It represents a person who has a situation resting upon shaky foundations. When the realisation hits home, all comes crashing down. This can feel abrupt, like a rude awakening. Yet, when the dust settles, they will see that this is an opportunity to rebuild.

The number **sixteen** within this card reduces to the number seven. This represents a spiritual awakening of the seven-chakra system.

Element: Fire

GENERAL READING

In general, the Tower card warns you that abrupt change is about to take place. Your world may be turned upside down by chaos but know that a shift in perception will allow you to expand. You won't appreciate this now, but in time, you will understand that you have gained wisdom from the experience you have endured.

Whether a breakdown in a relationship, a life-changing upheaval, or the sudden loss of a job is on the horizon, this is your chance to start over.

WORK READING

In work circumstances, the Tower card can symbolise unwanted change, such as being fired or demoted, a forced adjustment, or an unpredicted redundancy. This may feel shocking, terrifying, and totally out of the blue.

If you are seeking work, then an unexpected offer may be on the cards. Look for the Page of Cups or the Ace of Cups in the spread for validation.

If you are asking if you will get a particular job or if you should take a job offer, the answer is no. Things are not what they seem. Stay put.

LOVE READING

In love readings, the Tower can indicate breaking apart and the shattering of dreams. If a relationship is being put to the test, you will soon find how firm your foundations are. Home truths or shocking revelations may suddenly come to light. Remember that you deserve only the best; even though your world has fallen apart, you will heal and move on. You will get over it, dear one.

If you are asking how a person sees you romantically, then take this card as confirmation that you are perceived in a sexual tone. Just be aware that this person may only have their own needs and agendas in mind.

FINANCIAL READING

From a financial viewpoint, the Tower card forewarns you that things are not as they seem. There are illusions afoot. Perhaps a con artist is attempting to get their hands on your retirement fund, or you are about to sign a financial agreement without reading the small print. It would be wise to wait before making commitments at this time. Use discernment.

Many positive surrounding cards can indicate a cash windfall arriving out of the blue.

SPIRITUALITY READING

Spiritually speaking, the Tower card suggests that you are about to have a breakthrough within your psychic development. See the crown as your crown chakra awakening as it is struck with the wisdom light of the Divine. Make sure you remain grounded as you enjoy this period of bliss.

WELL-BEING READING

Well-being related, the Tower card asks you to slow down. This card isn't here to terrify you but to warn you that you could end up on a slippery downward slope if you continue to ignore warning signs regarding your health and well-being.

If you have been overstretched, you may have an eruption of emotions. You may suddenly realise that what you thought you wanted no longer satisfies you. This is all good. It's growth.

Very rarely, this card can manifest as an accident, indicating a hospital trip, for example.

ASSOCIATED KEYPHRASES
Upheaval
Chaos
A big change
An epiphany
Radical information coming to light
A spiritual awakening
Unforeseen events
Being unprepared

17 THE STAR

The Star card represents inspiration. The person it speaks of has been to hell and back, yet a glimmer of hope still burns within them. The worst is now over, and they are entering a period of healing and restoration. The scales are now coming back into balance. Let the good times roll!

This card is numbered **seventeen**. This reduces to eight, signifying eternity, youth, and the arrival of good fortune.

Element: Air

GENERAL READING

In general, the Star is one of the most beautiful cards in the deck. It ushers in a time of healing and restored hope. This is a very lucky time, so follow your dreams and take inspired action. If you have had a tough time of late, know this is over. Good things are finally coming your way.

A blessing is soon to be yours, so make a wish. Ask, and you will receive.

WORK READING

In work circumstances, the Star is a great omen. If you have recently applied for a new job or a promotion or are starting a new business venture, this card indicates great success is on the horizon.

If you are employed, you are being recognised for your brilliance. You stand out from the crowd, and others look to you for inspiration. Keep shining like the star that you are.

LOVE READING

In love readings, the Star can indicate a relationship in a dreamy new phase. You feel aligned and destined to meet as if it were "written in the stars."

If you have just gone through a rocky patch, this is a welcomed card indicating that calmer times are ahead. You are now healing and are both singing from the same song sheet.

If you are single, remain hopeful; someone worth waiting for will arrive in the near future.

FINANCIAL READING

From a financial viewpoint, the Star card promises that you can manifest your dreams into reality. Everything that you ever wanted is within reach. Just remember to meet the universe halfway. Apathy can keep abundance locked into the future.

This is a great time to take positive action steps and invest.

SPIRITUALITY READING

Spiritually speaking, the Star shows that you are a person of great faith. You have successfully navigated through a challenge and broke a karmic cycle. Congratulations! Your little light continued to shine even during the dark times, and now you are coming through the other side. You feel inspired, renewed, and vibrant.

You may have an affinity with the stars. Connect to Star beings to access ancient wisdom.

WELL-BEING READING

Well-being related, the Star restores your peace and contentment after a challenging period. You have been through a lot and now you are coming out the other side. If you have been unwell, expect to make a miraculous recovery. There may be a lot to process but healing is underway.

Your Divine guardians are so proud of you and have never left your side while you weathered the storm. Give thanks for the new energy that is available to you now. This will increase your blessings and renew your sense of well-being.

ASSOCIATED KEYPHRASES
Hope
A time of healing
Make a wish
Calmer times are ahead
Very good luck
Count your lucky stars
A promise of better days
A miracle takes place

18 THE MOON

The Moon card represents a person who is either exploring the great mystery or is totally baffled by it. During the darkness of night, visibility is limited. This is when we must trust our instincts, as things are not as they seem in the external world. Clarity will come along with the new day.

This card is number **eighteen**. Reduced to nine, it reflects the darkest hour before dawn. After enduring the long cold night, distortions and discomfort are at their peak. Relax; the sun is about to rise bringing you the answers you seek.

Element: Water

GENERAL READING

In general, the Moon card presents itself when there is a sense of mystery in the air. There is a need for clarity. Perhaps you are not sure where you stand with someone. Maybe confusion has arisen internally, and you're no longer sure what you want or need.

This is a good time to go within and reassess your values. If you feel you have swayed off course, plan to get back onto the straight and narrow. Trust your gut despite how things appear on the surface—they are not what they seem.

WORK READING

In work circumstances, the Moon card isn't a great card to pull. You may be unhappy with your current job and could be considering finding something else. This is not an easy decision, and you will likely feel torn. The source of your unhappiness is not the job itself but rather a negative influence within it. There may be bitching, gossiping, and backbiting. Pull away and invoke psychic protection.

If you are seeking work, take some time to dream about what you would love to do. Use your imagination.

This card can sometimes represent working night shifts.

LOVE READING

In love readings, the Moon card indicates some level of miscommunication. Perhaps you and your partner are not on the same page. Seeking a guidance councillor may be beneficial to help you to open up honest conversations.

This card does sometimes reveal deception. Use supporting cards to clarify if and what your partner is keeping from you. It could be an embarrassing health issue or hiding a shameful debt. Rather than intentionally harming you, perhaps your partner feels they are shielding you from pain somehow. If you suspect your partner has been lying or sneaking around, trust your instincts and look out for odd behaviour. More information will soon come to light.

If you are asking how someone feels about you, this card means they will not reveal their true feelings to you. They are either too confused or not in a position to admit it.

FINANCIAL READING

From a financial viewpoint, the Moon card warns you to tread with caution. Wait before you sign contracts or lend out money. Things are not what they seem. Protect your passwords. Be aware of con artists. There could be a sting in the tail.

SPIRITUALITY READING

Spiritually speaking, the Moon card indicates a deeply spiritual time. Your intuition is sharp, and your psychic powers are increasing.

Pay attention to your dreams. Important messages from your subconscious mind are coming to you during sleep. If you have dreamt of a deceased loved one, this card confirms that this was more than a dream; it was a visitation.

WELL-BEING READING

Well-being related, the Moon asks you to put yourself first and learn to say no to others' demands, or you will later feel resentful and tired. Worry may be affecting your sleep. If you have been feeling anxious, try to rationalise your fears.

You are sensitive to other people's energy at this very psychic time. Cut cords to keep your energy clear and stay grounded.

Your menstrual cycle may be making you or a woman you know feel emotional and overwhelmed with hormones. Take time to rest. Be compassionate.

ASSOCIATED KEYPHRASES

Facing your fears
Use your intuition
Prophetic dreams
Illusions
Being in the dark
Cycles and patterns
Fantasies running away with you
Confusion

19 THE SUN

The Sun is one of the most positive cards in the deck. It reflects a person who chooses to see the good in all things. This is a fun, warm-hearted person. Their energy is attractive and vibrant. Everyone loves to be touched by the warm rays of the sun.

This card is number **nineteen**. This reduces to one and reflects the happy feelings of this card and feeling at one.

Element: Fire

GENERAL READING

In general, the Sun card brings light and blessings to any situation. Creative solutions and a renewed enthusiasm for life now make worries a thing of the past. You can let go, relax, and enjoy this time of pleasure and contentment.

WORK READING

In work circumstances, the Sun card is a great omen. It denotes that you are aligned with your powerful inner masculine energies. This manifests as great focus, strong willpower, and an incredible determination to succeed.

If you are currently in work, enjoy this time of increased energy. You have an abundance of brilliant ideas and strategies. Your upbeat attitude inspires your peers. You are an inspiration.

If you recently applied for a job, this card indicates that good news is on the horizon! Anything you put your mind to now will be a brilliant success.

LOVE READING

In love readings, the Sun card ushes in a time of contentment. If you are in a relationship, things are going well. Authenticity is important to you, and it feels great to be with someone who encourages you to be yourself. Your relationship is honest, open, and fun. There could be talk of deepening your commitments by marriage or starting a family.

If you are single, you are happy within yourself. Your bubbly personality attracts others, meaning if you are looking, you will soon draw someone in with your warmth.

FINANCIAL READING

From a financial viewpoint, the Sun card indicates a time when anything is possible. The sky is the limit regarding what you can achieve. Investments are blossoming around you. There are opportunities to grow your finances. This is a great time to buy a new home or invest.

SPIRITUALITY READING

Spiritually speaking, the Sun is the card of enlightenment. You may have been through a rebirth of sorts, and now you are successfully through the other side. You feel empowered and reborn. There is a sense of clarity and joy within you. It feels so good to live in the moment.

You are a beacon of hope to others. Keep shining your light.

WELL-BEING READING

Well-being related, the Sun is the most assuring card. Your health has improved, or health-related answers have come to light so that true healing can occur. You are inspired to continue improving your health and well-being and are on the right track.

Continue this positive attitude, and you can enjoy feeling energised and whole. You may feel inclined to take a relaxing holiday.

ASSOCIATED KEYPHRASES
Clarity
Increased joy
A sense of freedom
Happiness
Your idea will be a success
Optimism
Authenticity
Loving life

20 JUDGEMENT

The Judgement card symbolises a person eager for change. A deep inner calling has propelled them into reviewing all areas of their life. What has not been working can no longer be ignored or tolerated. Personal fulfilment is now a priority.

This card is number **twenty.** Reduced to the number two, we see the choice of two pathways ahead.

Element: Fire

GENERAL READING

In general, the Judgement card brings in epiphanies and realisations often accompanied by a sense of urgency for change. You may feel you have wasted time on a person or project that no longer bears fruit. Remember the saying, "Don't be afraid to start over. This time, you are not starting from scratch; you are starting with experience."

You are now ready to seek a new path that will bring you joy. The attitude of this card is, "You live only once."

WORK READING

In work circumstances, the Judgement card suggests you are yet to find your true calling. Trust all is well; your Divine purpose is seeking you. An appraisal or review of your work will help you to gain perspective. If you feel the urge to walk a new pathway, go ahead! Allow your soul to lead the way.

LOVE READING

In love readings, the Judgement card asks you to be honest about your relationships. You may feel you are not on the same page as your partner. It has come to your attention that you have grown apart, and your values may have changed. You seek only complete honesty and integrity.

It's time to decide if you can realign or if it's time to part ways. Accept the past and learn from your mistakes.

If you are single, perhaps an experience in the past hurt you so deeply that you are too afraid to let anyone in. Like the souls in the card, open your arms and accept your destiny.

This card frequently appears in readings during Venus retrograde, a time when ex-lovers return from your past. Will you transcend the trappings of Samsara or continue to repeat the cycle?

FINANCIAL READING

From a financial viewpoint, the Judgement card asks you to take charge and assess the situation. If you are in debt, you are now ready to resolve this. You are motivated and see things clearly. Seek appropriate advice and make a plan moving forward.

Hire a life coach to help you change how you feel about money. A newly refined version of yourself is in the making.

SPIRITUALITY READING

Spiritually speaking, the Judgement card says that your spiritual higher self is whispering to you, longing to be acknowledged. This may manifest in synchronicity or a deep sense of wonder about the mystery of life itself.

You are being called to fulfil your soul contracts. Explore your curiosities; they will lead you in the right direction.

WELL-BEING READING

Well-being related, the Judgement card requires you to look closely at your health. You cannot put this off any longer. You may feel as though the past is catching up with you.

If you want to prevent the foundations for disease, now is the time to get your proverbial house in order. Take control. Choose health.

ASSOCIATED KEYPHRASES
A wake-up call
A spiritual calling
Announcements
Review your life
The past revisiting you
A realisation
A compelling desire
Changing your course of path

21 THE WORLD

The World card makes an appearance when a person is feeling accomplished. They have come to the end of a chapter and have successfully achieved whatever they set out to complete. This is a fabulous time that foresees great success.

The World card is number **twenty-one.** This number reduces to three and represents unity of mind, body, and spirit.

Element: Earth

GENERAL READING

In general, the World card denotes the successful completion of a project. This is a brilliant time when you feel accomplished and on top of the world. Bask in the limelight and enjoy the fruits of your labour.

A new journey is about to begin.

WORK READING

In work circumstances, the World card shows that your career is going incredibly well. Perhaps you have just completed a training course that has laid solid foundations for your future. Maybe you have received a promotion or even retired. You have shifted ranks or jumped up the career ladder.

There is a gentle sense of authority about you because you are so highly valued and experienced. Be confident that all your hard work has paid off.

This card gives a big yes to any job-related questions. Good news is on the horizon.

LOVE READING

In love readings, the World card says someone thinks the world of you. Take steps to maintain balance within relationships, as you tend to get carried away. Don't make someone else the centre of your world and revolve only around them. Equally, this can be a little reminder to consider your partner's needs. Maybe you are the one that has been putting yourself first.

This can be a wonderful card if you keep your feet on the ground and your heart open.

If you are single, this card can indicate that you will meet your future partner while travelling. Perhaps your future partner will be from another country.

FINANCIAL READING

From a financial viewpoint, the World card gives you permission to think big. There is potential for financial increase, so make the most of any opportunities that present themselves.

You have done enough research. It's time to act and believe in yourself.

SPIRITUALITY READING

Spiritually speaking, the World card indicates that you have just navigated your way through a life-changing lesson. Your spirit guides are cheering you on, celebrating you. You have come out on top and realise that everything has happened for your growth. Seeing things so clearly gives you great contentment and a sense of purpose.

The next step is to share what you have learned with others. Cosmic consciousness is yours.

WELL-BEING READING

Well-being related, the World card shows that you are at a personal high. You have manifested your desires; now it's time to wrap things up. You may be eager to get moving on to the next chapter.

Remember to savour the fruit of your labours and enjoy the journey, not just the destination. To keep up the momentum and feel invigorated, do something different. Travel and explore your options. Enjoy yourself.

This card indicates that you should be getting on top of health issues.

ASSOCIATED KEYPHRASES
A congratulations is in order
Feeling accomplished
On top of the world
The end of a cycle
Worldly success
Travel
A celebration
An achievement

CARD MEANINGS: THE MINOR ARCANA

THE SUIT OF WANDS

The suit of wands is governed by the element of fire. The power of fire resides in the direction of the south.

These cards represent situations that often revolve around careers, creative passions, and romance.

Fire, in its positive expression, is cleansing and energising. It can help you to clear away the energies of the past and evoke inspiration and passion. Use the powers of fire to stoke your inner desires, get creative at work, and reignite your relationships.

When expressed in its negative form, fire can be unpredictable, exhausting, and all-consuming. This manifests as rage, jumping the gun, being big-headed, and burning the candle at both ends.

To remedy excess fire, work with water. Get in touch with your emotions by journaling and conversing. Try listening to others to develop compassion. To increase your inner fire, get physical! Make love or undertake a high-intensity workout. Light candles and practice the fire breath.

The angels of the south fire are Archeia Aurora and Archangel Uriel. They govern the angels of light. Call them in to illuminate your path and inspire you along the way.

THE ACE OF WANDS

GENERAL READING

In general, the Ace of Wands is a great card that will bring excitement into any reading. This is a time of unlimited potential. From a romantic affair to a dazzling career opportunity, the world is your oyster.

Have confidence in your ideas. Follow your dreams and allow your passion to lead. Grab opportunities with both hands.

WORK READING

In work circumstances, the Ace of Wands denotes a new job, a promotion, or a fantastic money-making plan on the horizon. You have a wealth of ideas and must put them into action. If you are asking a career-related question, your answer is yes, yes, yes. Go for it!

It's time to level up! You are ready for this next stage in your career, and you deserve it. Follow what lights you up inside.

LOVE READING

In love readings, the Ace of Wands signifies great passion! If you are in a committed relationship, you are entering a period of harmony and are getting on well. There is a sense of renewal and contentment with each other.

If you are asking if someone has a romantic interest in you, this card says most certainly yes! The person you have in mind finds you incredibly attractive. There is a strong chemistry between you. Sparks may well be flying!

If you are single, then prepare for someone to intrigue you. You are about to have your head turned in a big way.

Remember that this card is sexual rather than romantic, meaning you will be in with a shot, but whether it leads anywhere or fizzles out will be revealed in time.

If you are asking if a lover has a wandering eye, then see this card as a testosterone-fuelled red-blooded male. Watch out for the Devil and the Seven of Swords for more confirmation of infidelity.

FINANCIAL READING

From a financial viewpoint, the Ace of Wands brings you the gift of opportunity. You are now entering a period of good luck. This card may manifest as a gift, bonus, or windfall. Yet again, it may be the archetypal Magician handing you his wand and saying, "Make it happen."

This is a great time, and you have a real buzz inside you. Tap into this energy to drive your goals to fruition.

Sometimes, this card manifests as a house move. Look out for the Four of Wands in the spread to reinforce this meaning.

SPIRITUALITY READING

Spiritually speaking, the Ace of Wands brings you a kundalini awakening. This could be a very spiritual time for you. Cultivate a practice to explore your interior landscape. Your inner guru is awakening.

Use movement and breathwork to awaken the inner serpent. Study the tantric arts. Successfully raise the energy throughout your chakra column, and a rebirth in consciousness will be yours.

WELL-BEING READING

Well-being related, the Ace of Wands indicates that you are feeling invigorated. Your energy levels are at an all-time high. You are contented with your newfound inspiration keeping you upbeat.

Remember to keep your feet on the ground and take a balanced approach. Ensure you get enough sleep and remember to eat. All the excitement might just have you getting carried away, and we don't want you running out of steam.

ASSOCIATED KEYPHRASES
The arrival of incredible news
Your passion is ignited
Career expansion
Sexual attraction
Creative ideas
Enthusiasm
An exciting new beginning
Fertility

THE TWO OF WANDS

GENERAL READING

In general, the Two of Wands arises when you have a decision to make. You may be second-guessing yourself. Is your idea really going to work? Tap into the inspiration that you had at the start of your project, then allow yourself time to contemplate.

This is a good time to pause before you proceed onward. There is more insight to be gained. Perhaps someone can help point you in the right direction.

WORK READING

In work circumstances, the Two of Wands augurs a time of increased support. Don't be afraid to seek a second opinion. Maybe a coach or an accountability partner would help you to remain focused. A fresh set of eyes will work wonders for your career.

Keep planning the next steps and figure out how to expand. There is room for growth.

LOVE READING

In love readings, the Two of Wands symbolises someone weighing their options. This card could, of course, represent your own feelings. Maybe you feel at a bit of a crossroads and are just seeing how things go.

You may be questioning another person's intentions. If they are blowing hot and cold, you will feel like you don't know where you stand with them. You deserve better than this. Do not settle for someone who is keeping their options open. Actions speak louder than words. Watch how they act. Therein lies your answer.

If you are single and asking if you will meet someone in the future, the answer is yes. You have learned from your past and have higher expectations. Someone worth waiting for will come along.

FINANCIAL READING

From a financial viewpoint, the Two of Wands asks you to bide your time. Your investments so far are solid, but it would serve you well to investigate your options. Hire a professional to help you run over your accounts. It seems there are some ways in which you can cut back and save if you get the proper guidance.

You may be waiting for a business to get started. Make a solid plan that you can follow and take charge of.

You are coming closer to your goals.

SPIRITUALITY READING

Spiritually speaking, the Two of Wands manifests as your angels and guides coming to say hello. Your spiritual team are trying to get your attention right now. You may have noticed signs and synchronicities. Take time out to meditate and journal. The information they want to reveal will help you walk the path of least resistance.

Know that you are never alone. Spiritual guides are waiting to offer you love, healing, and support.

WELL-BEING READING

Well-being related, the Two of Wands urges you to stop what you are doing and invest some quality time in yourself. You have expended a tremendous amount of energy as of late, and it's time to replenish.

If you are indecisive and unsure how to proceed, know it's just because you are tired. Perhaps you could do with someone to lean on for a change. Reach out for support where you can.

ASSOCIATED KEYPHRASES
In the planning process
A partnership
The world is your oyster
Get organised
A desire to travel
Explore your options
Choosing the next pathway
Contemplating

THE THREE OF WANDS

GENERAL READING

In general, the Three of Wands is a wonderful card to draw that signals achievement. When it arrives, you can relax, knowing that your hard work has paid off. You have established yourself well and made great progress. This was a successful venture. Take a moment to enjoy what you have created.

This card can sometimes indicate upcoming travel.

WORK READING

In work circumstances, the Three of Wands is a great card. A congratulations may be in order! If you have applied for a new position or are awaiting a contract, you will soon hear good news.

You have made massive headway in building your personal empire. Now that you are at the top of your game, you may feel ready to branch out and level up. Pat yourself on the back for your efforts. Your incoming abundance is well deserved. Good for you.

This card can sometimes indicate work overseas, working in the travel industry, or branching out (moving from self-employed to a limited company, for example).

LOVE READING

In love readings, the Three of Wands will need further cards to clarify its meaning. On one hand, it may indicate a person who isn't interested in a serious relationship. Their mind is focused on travel or career advancement.

Sometimes, three signifies that "three's a crowd." Perhaps there is more than one option on the table.

In its most positive form, this card can show a firmly established relationship going from strength to strength. Look for the Two or Ten of Cups cards in the same reading.

Maybe this card is pointing to a long-distance relationship or a holiday romance. Be sure to study surrounding cards and trust your intuition on how this card relates to your reading.

FINANCIAL READING

From a financial viewpoint, the Three of Wands is a fantastic card to receive, signifying that your investments will multiply. So far, you may have only seen a fraction of a return on your stakes. You should feel very excited knowing that the best is yet to come.

You have an opportunity for massive growth. Be confident and go for it. You are well prepared.

Any partnerships entered into at this time will be supportive and trustworthy. Allow others to drive your vision even further afield.

SPIRITUALITY READING

Spiritually speaking, the Three of Wands brings in the energy of harmony. You are seeing life from the eyes of your soul and this enables you to perceive the bigger picture. You understand that you are part of a collective consciousness, and what you give out comes back to you.

You are supported, and you know it. It feels so good to have this connection to all that is. Share the wisdom of your soul. Guide others onto the path of light.

WELL-BEING READING

Well-being related, the Three of Wands brings you strength. Everything you need to improve your health is available, whether appropriate healthcare, answers from investigations and tests, or the sheer willpower to commit to a healthier lifestyle.

All that you require is at hand and healing is on its way. Relax knowing that a full recovery is possible.

ASSOCIATED KEYPHRASES
Being committed to your vision
What you want is on its way
Waiting for results
Planning for the future
Making great progress
Dream big
Travel
Business expansion

THE FOUR OF WANDS

GENERAL READING

In general, the Four of Wands represents all the good vibes. You are feeling blessed, supported, and accepted by your family or friends. Knowing you are an integral part of the community gives you a deep sense of peace and fulfilment.

This is a time of laughter, abundance, and love. There is a celebration coming, and you will have a wonderful time. You will create memories that you will cherish forever. Let the good times roll.

WORK READING

In work circumstances, the Four of Wands may be inviting you to a lovely new workplace.

Generally, there is a good atmosphere at work with a great team that supports you well. Colleagues are more likely to feel like friends or even family. You feel at home where you are.

This card can also indicate working from home.

LOVE READING

In love readings, the Four of Wands will uplift your spread. This card brings a surge of fresh energy into your relationships. You are entering a period in which you feel more deeply connected. Your relationship is safe. You can trust your partners' commitment; this relationship means everything to them.

Perhaps a baby, fur baby, or new home is on the horizon. Your relationship is strengthening, and your family is your whole world.

If you are asking about the outcome of a relationship, this card says you will move in together.

If you have recently endured a breakup, this card can indicate that an estranged lover will return. See other cards for clarity, looking out for the Two or Ten of Cups.

FINANCIAL READING

From a financial viewpoint, the Four of Wands brings you comfort, safety, and stability. You should have surplus income now, but it would be wise to remember your roots and anyone that supported you along the way.

Now is the perfect time to start a new business, buy a home, or invest. Get building for the future. This is the card of lasting things.

SPIRITUALITY READING

Spiritually speaking, the Four of Wands signifies that you are ready for a fresh start. You have learned to forgive and let go so that you can walk freely from past restraints.

Your fresh perspective attracts new energy and opportunities. Your spiritual team is celebrating you and cheering you on with support. They recognise how far you have come. You are spiritually maturing, and life looks more beautiful than ever.

Perhaps there is a spiritual community that can teach you the mysteries of the old ways, the homecoming of the soul.

WELLBEING READING

Well-being related, the Four of Wands suggests that you are in a great place mentally and life is good. All is well in your personal life. This, in turn, boosts your health and vitality.

If you have been unwell, this card brings stability and a return to health. If a family member is ill in hospital, this card indicates that they will recover and return home. This is the card of miracles and blessings where anything can happen.

ASSOCIATED KEYPHRASES
Family
A celebration
Purchasing or moving to a new house
Feeling settled and contented
Someone moves in, or a baby is born
Parties, reunions, and get-togethers
Relocating
Home is where the heart is

THE FIVE OF WANDS

GENERAL READING

In general, the Five of Wands talks about struggles and disagreements that are on the horizon. There is a sense of hostility between parties. Emotions could be running high, and misunderstandings can easily occur right now.

It's important to take a step back and evaluate the situation. Is this really worth getting involved in? Are you making a mountain out of a molehill? Clear your mind and figure things out. If you can come from a place of clarity, it's possible to prevent this card from reaching its peak.

Use the positioning of the cards (or pull a clarifier) to determine which area of life the conflict is arising.

WORK READING

In work circumstances, the Five of Wands may find you on harsh footing. Usually, this card denotes conflict and tension in the air. There could be intense competition around you, and colleagues might be fighting for a place at the top. This may leave you feeling like you must jockey for your position and constantly prove your worth. It is an exhausting situation to be in.

Slow down; you don't need to hustle. See if you can make amends or compromise. Put your feet in someone else's shoes. Failing that, keep yourself to yourself. Don't give bullies any of your energy to contend with.

If you are unemployed, it may be that you are struggling daily just to get by.

LOVE READING

In love readings, the Five of Wands represents silly little squabbles through full-blown feuds. You and your partner may have differing opinions, and this clash in values is causing a negative cycle of tit for tat. If your partner is constantly nagging, try to see their point of view. Perhaps by opening up and laying down your sword, you'll be able to see eye to eye.

If you are single, take this time to get yourself straightened out. It's unlikely you have time for a relationship right now.

FINANCIAL READING

From a financial viewpoint, the Five of Wands has you frustrated over money. Perhaps you are in a disagreement over an injustice or maybe you have been arguing with someone over cash. Try and let go of any anger that you may be harbouring towards yourself or others.

You may be feeling taken advantage of or ripped off but let go of the victim attitude. Instead, use the energy wasted on worry to come up with solutions to create abundance. It may be time to put your foot down with freeloaders.

SPIRITUALITY READING

Spiritually speaking, the Five of Wands suggests you have been through a hard time. You may feel as though you are being tested right now. Frustrating circumstances keep creeping up. You may have wondered whether these situations are karmic. Notice what patterns are playing out and ask for guidance on reinstating peace.

WELL-BEING READING

Well-being related, the Five of Wands indicates that you could be experiencing minor health niggles. Tiredness and stress may be taking all your energy away, but if you focus on yourself and make well-being a priority, it will be well worth it. Get the support you need—ground scattered energy. Treat yourself with love.

This card can denote a course of medication that helps you battle an illness.

ASSOCIATED KEYPHRASES
Conflict
Anger
Hurdles and Challenges
Competition
Strife
Obstacles
Struggle
Tired of fighting

THE SIX OF WANDS

GENERAL READING

In general, the Six of Wands is an incredible card to receive. It indicates a positive time when you can truly stand in your power and admire what you have created. You are at an advantage over your peers, making this a very successful time regardless of your enquiry.

Your vision is clear, and you have the internal hunger and stamina to go the extra mile. Your light is shining brightly. You have done a good job.

WORK READING

In work circumstances, the Six of Wands denotes good news. If you have recently applied for a new position of work, then success will be yours.

If you are working, then you are making a strong impression. People look up to you. You are highly competent—so much so that you will soon likely rank in a leadership position. Your talents will be recognised by your team. You are an asset to any business.

Keep up the good work and remember to congratulate yourself for your excellence.

LOVE READING

In love readings, the Six of Wands asks for balance. Have you been smitten with someone? Are you observing a person through rose-tinted glasses? This card indicates that you may have put someone on a pedestal, and while this is a positive card, it serves as a reminder that your needs are as important as anybody else's.

If this is a romance enquiry, then the answer is YES. Your love interest really likes you. You hold the power to attain whatever or whoever you desire. Just make sure you make obvious whom you find attractive, as they may feel you are a little out of their league!

FINANCIAL READING

From a financial viewpoint, the Six of Wands is a great card. Take this as an omen that you will come out on top. With your positive attitude and perseverance, you will manifest the abundance you want. This is a perfect time to invest, apply for jobs, and put yourself out there.

This card foresees an increase in profits, and opportunities abound.

SPIRITUALITY READING

Spiritually speaking, the Six of Wands suggests you need to ground your energy. You have expanded exponentially. Remember to slow down and integrate what you have learned.

Your optimistic energy is infectious, so don't be surprised if everyone wants to get close to you! People will want to know your secret to success. Perhaps you are about to assume the role of a leader or teacher. You are ready! Just maintain humility, and don't let all this positive recognition go to your head.

WELL-BEING READING

Well-being related, the Six of Wands is an assuring card. If you have had any health issues, you should soon be feeling bright and on top of the world again. Feelings of happiness and contentment awaken within you. Embrace this joyful time.

ASSOCIATED KEYPHRASES
Victory
Success
Being acknowledged
Coming out on top
Be confident in yourself
You are at your peak
A milestone
Good news is coming

THE SEVEN OF WANDS

GENERAL READING

In general, the Seven of Wands denotes a period of struggle. You may feel like attacks (challenges) are coming in from all angles, and you must continually defend yourself. However, this card does have a positive aspect.

Despite these annoyances, you do have the strength to successfully conquer whatever you are facing. So, stand up for your beliefs with confidence.

WORK READING

In work circumstances, the Seven of Wands may find you with your tail in a spin. Your to-do list is constantly increasing, leaving you wondering how on Earth you will ever get on top of things. You may feel like you are being pulled in many directions, and people are demanding your attention. If this is so, see where you can delegate tasks. Take a step back from taking on more. It's ok to say no.

There could be some jealousy around you. Perhaps someone is trying to overthrow you! Stand your ground. You are in the strongest position. Remember, a little competition can keep you on top of your game.

If you are looking for work, you could have had quite a few knockbacks. Hang on in there and keep on searching. Your perseverance will pay off eventually.

LOVE READING

In love readings, the Seven of Wands is not a good card to draw, for it indicates that you may be going through a rocky patch. This card frequently appears when people feel they must keep explaining themselves to their partners. It is tiresome to be constantly on the defence. If your partner is stressed, you could find yourself in the firing line. Seek support.

If this card pairs up with the Three of Cups, the Devil, the High Priestess, or the Lovers, another person may be trying to entice your lover to stray.

When single, this can be a great card! Maybe you have so many admirers you are swatting offers away. If not, perhaps low self-esteem is preventing you from putting yourself out there. Practice building your confidence.

FINANCIAL READING

From a financial viewpoint, the Seven of Wands brings challenges you can handle. It may be one of those times when you need to keep forking out for one thing or another. Yet this card doesn't foresee financial ruin.

Be pragmatic, take a practical approach, and tackle your situation head-on. Deal with things now, and you will be able to regain balance. Bury your head in the sand, and you will soon end up fighting a losing battle.

SPIRITUALITY READING

Spiritually speaking, the Seven of Wands reminds you to invoke psychic protection. Psychically, you have left yourself vulnerable to being drained by energy vampires. An ill-intended rival could have well provoked recent misfortune.

Clear and shield your aura, your home, and your property. Ask a higher force to make yourself invisible to adversaries.

WELL-BEING READING

Well-being related, the Seven of Wands has you feeling all wound up, and you may be experiencing symptoms of intense stress. You could be enduring a period of insomnia or heightened anxiety with excess adrenalin, leaving you jittery and overwhelmed. You have the power to get on top of this with professional help and relaxation.

If you are battling a very serious illness at this time, this card assures you that you will come out on top. You will win this battle.

ASSOCIATED KEYPHRASES
Feeling defensive
Being on guard
Stand your ground
Under attack
Competition
Feeling as though you have bitten off more than you can chew
Choose your battles wisely
Commit to your vision

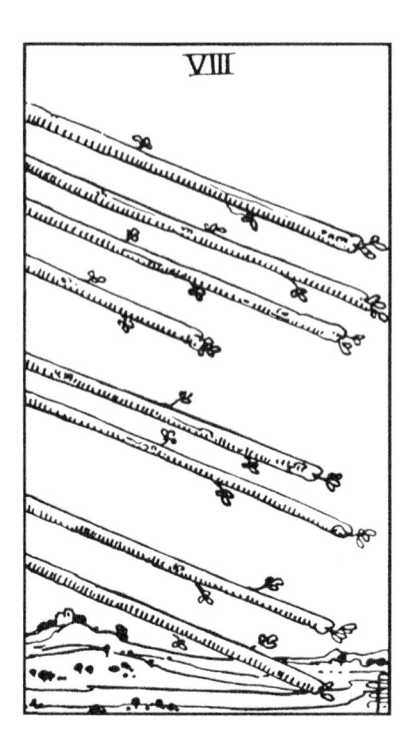

THE EIGHT OF WANDS

GENERAL READING

In general, the Eight of Wands reassures you that you are on the right path. This is a busy period when events suddenly take flight. Delays are finally over, and previously closed doors now begin to open. Opportunities are coming thick and fast; you may need to think or act quickly. Follow your passion and trust that this is your time to fly high.

WORK READING

In work circumstances, the Eight of Wands is a positive sign. You have made great headway, and now your projects are taking shape. This is a time of expansion and rapid growth. Hold on to your hat!

If you are launching a new business or project, keep advancing. This could be a very successful venture.

If you are looking for work, this card reveals that something will come up sooner than you think. This card can denote working abroad.

LOVE READING

In love readings, the Eight of Wands is a lovely card to draw. In fact, this card was once considered one of the romance cards, the wands depicting Cupid's arrows. If you are single, you might just find yourself being swept up in a whirlwind romance.

If you are taken, a sense of harmony surrounds you. You and your partner want the same things, and this brings you happiness and contentment.

FINANCIAL READING

From a financial viewpoint, the Eight of Wands brings you opportunities to increase your wealth. However, you may have to invest first before you see a return. Taking this risk may leave you feeling uncomfortable. It may seem as though you are haemorrhaging money right now, but so long as you have a strategy, things will work out. Ensure you are totally invested in your idea, then give it everything you've got.

SPIRITUALITY READING

Spiritually speaking, the Eight of Wands asks you to remain grounded and consolidate your energy. Your psychic abilities are really ramping up, and while this is very exciting, you must maintain balance and come back down to Earth.

This is a great time to explore the psychic clairs, astral travel, lucid dreaming, and any other metaphysical abilities. Just be sure to close down your psychic centres efficiently afterwards.

WELL-BEING READING

Well-being related, the Eight of Wands brings you vitality. At last, you have the energy and the motivation to make positive changes in your life.

It feels so good to be fully on board with yourself; this motivates you to stick to your plans. Emotionally, you feel supported and on the right path, boosting your confidence even further.

Perhaps a holiday would provide a good opportunity to refill your cup to keep the momentum going.

ASSOCIATED KEYPHRASES
Swiftness
Approaching a goal
Your intention has been cast
Travel
Be patient; your dreams are coming true
Conclusions are being made
Direct communication
Taking action

THE NINE OF WANDS

GENERAL READING

In general, the Nine of Wands arrives in a reading when you have been fighting a long, hard challenge. You are feeling exhausted, but you have not been defeated. Although you are weary, know that you are almost at the finish line. Don't give up now.

WORK READING

In work circumstances, the Nine of Wands denotes opposition. You may have had to stand up for yourself and defend your position. On this occasion, you are encouraged to fight for what is right. Protect your idea and defend your name.

Whatever you are standing for is on the verge of resolution. You'll recover anything you've lost in this battle, and your determination to win will see you through.

If you are looking for work, you may have been searching for a while. Hang on in there.

LOVE READING

In love readings, the Nine of Wands has you on your guard. Does someone have you feeling as though you need to watch your back as if they are trying to trip you up? Perhaps you are the one who is suspicious of your partner. You may be at the end of your tether, but this card reminds you (without condoning) that hurt people, hurt people. Can you open up and work with a therapist to get through this?

If you are single, you might be wondering if you will ever meet the right one. You have had your fair share of heartbreak, and as a result, you find it very difficult to trust. You are constantly on guard. Heal your past. Learn to leave it behind you like the man in the card.

FINANCIAL READING

From a financial viewpoint, the Nine of Wands reminds you to protect your finances! Keep an eye on your spending and be prepared. For example, do you need to start a pension? Have you got home insurance? Get a plan in place so your earnings are safely tied up for your future.

SPIRITUALITY READING

Spiritually speaking, the Nine of Wands has you feeling weary. Recent events may have been so harsh that even your faith has been challenged. You have the strength to get through this. As the saying goes, "when it's hardest to pray, pray hardest". Reconnect to the Divine for support. Hang in there, and you will get your second wind.

WELL-BEING READING

Well-being related, the Nine of Wands foresees you successfully conquering health challenges. You may have been through a difficult period and are now feeling exhausted. Heal and restore your energy. Remain optimistic, expect to make a full recovery, and try not to worry.

This card can represent someone who suffers with tension headaches and migraines.

ASSOCIATED KEYPHRASES

Facing challenges
Hang on in there
You have endured a long battle
Standing up for yourself
Too many demands on your time
Feeling defeated
Protect yourself
See things through to the end

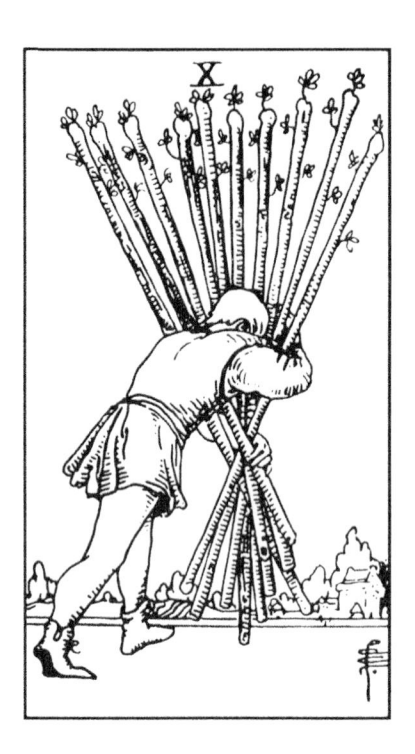

THE TEN OF WANDS

GENERAL READING

In general, the Ten of Wands says that you have been working incredibly hard and are exhausted. You have become laden with responsibilities, which is becoming hard to bear. From excessive physical work to meeting the emotional demands of others, you know you cannot go on any longer without it being to your detriment.

WORK READING

In work circumstances, the Ten of Wands asks you to lighten your load. You have probably become the go-to person from whom peers seek support, but you have already taken on too much. Talk to your employer and see where you can implement boundaries.

If you run your own business, you may have more customers than you can manage. Perhaps you are assuming the role of several people. Get staff or trainees to help you regain balance.

When unemployed, this card suggests that you're worried about how you will support yourself.

LOVE READING

In love readings, the Ten of Wands can indicate that your relationship is arduous work. Perhaps your partner has had their own struggles, and you have had to step up and support them for a while. It has been an uphill battle, and you are wondering how much more you can take. You have the strength to continue, but you must realise that this will come at a cost. You must set a long-term plan in place to see the light at the end of the tunnel.

If you are single, looking for love seems like hard work. Take a break from the dating game until you feel inspired again.

FINANCIAL READING

From a financial viewpoint, the Ten of Wands has you feeling burdened with bills, work, or responsibilities. Perhaps your finances are so overstretched that you feel like an elastic band about to snap. You are constantly slogging and juggling to make ends meet. You likely have dependants relying upon you for financial care and support, so dropping the ball is not an option.

Yet it's not all doom and gloom. There is a solution that you are not yet aware of. Share your struggles with others. They may look at things differently and come up with a solution.

SPIRITUALITY READING

Spiritually speaking, the Ten of Wands reminds you to have faith. You have been so busy with work that you have not made enough time for your spiritual practice. As a result, you now feel cut off from the Divine.

Remember that our creator never leaves our side. Ask for help. You are tired on every level. Take time to nourish your spirit.

WELL-BEING READING

Well-being related, the Ten of Wands says that you have not been taking good enough care of yourself. With all your commitments, your own needs have been cast onto the back burner. You are exhausted and need to put yourself first, or you are heading for burnout. You can only burn the candle at both ends for so long before it catches up with you.

Simplify your life. If you can afford it, hire a cleaner or babysitter to buy back some precious time to invest in yourself. You can't pour from an empty jug. Talk about your burdens with a person who you can trust.

This card can sometimes represent a person with a bad back.

ASSOCIATED KEYPHRASES
Being overburdened
Hard-working
An all-consuming situation
You are struggling
Not having enough time
A workaholic
Taking responsibility
The weight of the world on your shoulders

COURT CARDS:
THE WANDS ARCHETYPES

The following cards represent the archetypal personalities of the court cards in the suit of wands.

The wands or fire court cards mainly represent the personalities the querent is expressing or needs to align with to achieve their goal.

Wands sometimes (not always) represent those who are born under the star signs of Aries, Leo, and Sagittarius.

Wands people are creative, passionate, and crave freedom. They can represent artists, people who love to travel, or people you find sexually attractive (regardless of star sign). They can be fun, flirty, and impatient.

These cards often arise when you feel inspired and have a new ambition you want to sink your teeth into.

THE PAGE OF WANDS

GENERAL READING

In general, the Page of Wands has you feeling inspired. Interesting information or new ideas have come to light, and you are consumed with wonder and possibility. A career opportunity or creative project likely has you intrigued. This is an exciting time when following your passion could lead to something fruitful.

The Page of Wands can also represent a creative or fiery young person in your life. If you are worried about them, the solution lies in their ability to express themselves.

WORK READING

In work circumstances, the Page of Wands can indicate small positive changes are starting to take place. However modest, this is not something to be sniffed at. As the proverb says, "the mighty oaks from little acorns grow".

If you are unemployed, perhaps a part-time vacancy will open up. It may not be exactly what you were looking for, but it will get your foot in the door.

If you are currently employed, perhaps your workplace is considering placing you on a training course or is about to offer you an opportunity to expand.

Sometimes, this card represents a second job. If you have the time, a side hustle could be a great way to boost your income.

LOVE READING

In love readings, the Page of Wands can indicate that someone new has sparked your interest. This person is likely younger than you; at the very least, they make you feel young at heart. Joyful feelings awaken within you. You want to get to know this person more.

If you are committed, maybe your children are getting in the way of having quality time alone with your partner. Be sure to make time for affection to keep that romantic flame alive.

FINANCIAL READING

From a financial viewpoint, the Page of Wands brings you the opportunity to increase your income. This is not usually a massive raise, yet you will feel incredibly grateful for the extra abundance you are incurring. Money-making ideas are plenty.

SPIRITUALITY READING

Spiritually speaking, the Page of Wands encourages you to embrace your inner child. Get creative and use your imagination to polish your psychic gifts. This is a great time to delve into astral travel, creative writing, or channelled writing to explore your inner landscape.

WELL-BEING READING

Well-being related, the Page of Wands is a pleasant card to draw. It indicates that you are feeling quite cheerful. You are actively examining your life and have the enthusiasm to make changes and try new ways of doing things. You understand that happiness is your responsibility, and you are rolling up your sleeves and cultivating joy. It feels good to have the confidence to express your needs and wants.

Physically you are strong with an immense sense of vitality, making this a perfect time to take on an adventure!

ASSOCIATED KEYPHRASES
Starting a new project
Feeling intrigued
Closely examining something
Making plans
Feeling eager
Trying new things
Brilliant new ideas
Ready for an adventure

THE KNIGHT OF WANDS

GENERAL READING

In general, the Knight of Wands represents an amazing person who everyone wants to get to know. This is someone who is a lot of fun, the real-life-and-soul-of-the-party type. This Knight is regarded as the most attractive male of the deck. He oozes charisma and sex appeal.

If this Knight's qualities are speaking directly to you, they are encouraging you to have confidence and take charge. You can do this!

WORK READING

In work circumstances, the Knight of Wands says you have a revolutionary mind. You are ahead of the curve, trailblazing the pathway for others to follow. Your creative qualities are an asset to your work, and your peers can rely on you to come up with new ideas.

If you are self-employed, you are forthcoming and confident. With your passionate drive and laser focus on your goals, you will achieve great success. This is a busy time, perhaps with travel involved.

LOVE READING

In love readings, the Knight of Wands has varied interpretations. If you are single, be prepared to be swept off your feet by an incredibly charming person. Just don't fall in love too soon, as this Knight could whirl out of your life as quickly as he came in.

If you are in a committed relationship, this card indicates a strong sexual attraction is present. This relationship should be fuelled with fun and adventure.

The only downside to pulling this card in a relationship reading is when it is accompanied by the Devil, the Three of Cups, or the Seven of Swords. If anyone is going to cheat on you, it is your Knight of Fire!

FINANCIAL READING

From a financial viewpoint, the Knight of Wands ushers in a time of success. You have what it takes to make things happen, so if increased wealth is on your agenda, go for it. Tap into your creative skills for inspiration, and then take action. Use your charm and warm nature to create opportunities and supporters of your work. You know how to get your own way.

The Knight of Wands has an impulsive streak and can be inclined to take a gamble. Do your research before spending, and if your plans seem sound, then charge ahead.

SPIRITUALITY READING

Spiritually speaking, the Knight of Wands is inviting you on an adventure to take a break from the norm. If you are stuck in a rut, you will be feeling stifled and restless. Don't allow boredom to loom over you until you, initiate change. Explore unchartered waters and let off some steam. Feed your soul by experiencing all the wonderful facets of life.

WELL-BEING READING

Well-being related, the Knight of Wands brings you high energy. He is very athletic, and in a wellness reading, he questions your fitness levels. Perhaps you could push yourself a little more.

If you are suffering from anxiety, your guidance is to shake it off with exercise and movement.

ASSOCIATED KEYPHRASES
A romantic interest
Embarking upon an adventure
Take action
Being bold
Determination
Bravery
Feeling aligned with your purpose
Put yourself out there

THE QUEEN OF WANDS

GENERAL READING

In general, the Queen of Wands represents a popular, attractive woman. She is incredibly confident and has a real zest for life. This can represent someone you admire, a kind-hearted leader or an aspect of yourself.

Drawing this card indicates that you are perceived to have an idyllic life, someone who has it all. But the truth is, your resilience was forged through the fire of suffering. Like the mighty phoenix, you rose from the ashes, leaving past traumas behind.

WORK READING

In work circumstances, the Queen of Wands demands that you put yourself out there if you seek work. You are incredibly creative and hard-working; you just need an opportunity to shine.

If you have flitted back and forth between many jobs, you just need find your true calling. You are loyal and determined, so once passion has been ignited, there will be no stopping you.

If you work for yourself, your hobby likely became your full-time business. Your interest can soon fizzle out if you are not passionate about a project. You need the freedom to express yourself. You don't like to be pinned down.

LOVE READING

In love readings, the Queen of Wands is a great card to pull when asking how a romantic interest perceives you. You are warm-hearted and interesting, with a great sense of humour. Others find your energy sultry and magnetic; you have many admirers. If you are single, that's because you want to be.

The Queen of Wands is the irresistible woman in the deck, making her the obvious one to watch when looking for 'the other woman'. As always, drawing this card alone doesn't necessarily mean you should jump to this conclusion. Look for additional cheat cards in the spread, such as the Magician, the High Priestess, and the Seven of Swords, to bring more weight to any assumptions.

FINANCIAL READING

From a financial viewpoint, the Queen of Wands ushers in a fruitful time. You have the knowledge and the resources to successfully manifest abundance. You have laid your foundations in the world, and it's likely that you are already financially secure.

You like the finer things in life, so remember to cut your cloth; like most people, you too can overindulge from time to time. Keep a state of balance, and don't let a love of money take over your life.

SPIRITUALITY READING

Spiritually speaking, the Queen of Wands indicates that you are tuned in to the wisdom of your higher self. This is a lovely time when your creativity is overflowing and you have a strong sense of purpose.

Your energy field is healing to others; they may want to bask in your light. Because you are very empathic, people find it easy to open up to you. Remember to clear your space if you feel like you are absorbing harsh energies.

Perhaps you are a spiritual teacher, and people look up to you for guidance.

WELL-BEING READING

Well-being related, the Queen of Wands reminds you to adhere to the principle of give and take. Your high energy and enthusiasm mean you are often inclined to do more than your fair share. You are very efficient and like to get things done, but don't take on too much and later feel resentful.

Physically, you are strong and mentally, you feel very upbeat.

ASSOCIATED KEYPHRASES
Confidence
Ambition
Creativity
Hard-working
Having incredible vision
Adaptability
Leadership
Being independent

THE KING OF WANDS

GENERAL READING

In general, the King of Wands usually represents a male in your life or an aspect of yourself. This is a mature person who has a lot of life experience. Life is too short for nonsense; this person chooses to focus on what they feel is truly important.

If this card is talking directly towards you, you should feel quite accomplished with yourself. You have successfully navigated through many of life's challenges and have managed to come out on top. Your failures and victories have become valuable teaching aids to the benefit of others. Keep on paving the way.

WORK READING

In work circumstances, the King of Wands is a great card to draw. In work, you are well on your way up the career ladder. Leading and guiding others comes naturally to you. You are passionate and inquisitive, wanting to know everything about your craft. You are incredibly well-experienced and are regarded as an expert by peers. Yet you constantly seek to better yourself. You are quite the perfectionist.

If you are looking for work, seize the day. Someone with your skill set will be snapped up in no time.

LOVE READING

In love readings, the King of Wands denotes a loyal and passionate lover. If you are in a committed relationship, then you and your partner are fully invested in each other. You are a great team, but you also like to pursue your own interests. This relationship feels stable and safe yet is also spontaneous and fun. There is an intense physical attraction between you both.

If you are single, the King of Wands could soon sweep you off your feet. This is an incredibly attractive person who knows their own mind. You can expect more from this person than your average date. This person loves to travel and seeks adventure. You are in for a great time.

FINANCIAL READING

From a financial viewpoint, the King of Wands reminds you to gauge your bets from experience. You are wise to the pitfalls of investing and can assess whether chances are worth taking.

Overall, you should be feeling quite flush. Money comes easily because you are not afraid of hard work. You have great taste and a love of luxury.

SPIRITUALITY READING

Spiritually speaking, the King of Wands invites you to become one with the light. You have worked on your psychology, studied your ego, and are very much in touch with your soul. Your crown chakra is expanding, drawing in the wisdom teachings of the Divine Father. You are on the cusp of enlightenment. Stay humble.

WELL-BEING READING

Well-being related, the King of Wands is a great card. He arrives in your reading when you are feeling quite happy. Even though you have ambitions, you are contented with the phase you are at, leaving you at peace with how things are. Health and well-being are important to you. You like to look after yourself. Physically and mentally, you are strong and well.

ASSOCIATED KEYPHRASES

You are wise
Become a leader
You know what to do
Passionate
Focus
Do the right thing
You are experienced
Confidence

THE SUIT OF CUPS

The suit of cups is governed by the element of water. The power of water resides in the direction of the west.

The cups cards represent situations including love, relationships, and feelings.

In its positive expression, water is flowing, trusting, and caring. Water energy can help you to be loving towards yourself and others. Call in the power of water to clear your psychic centres and unveil your intuition.

When water is expressed in its negative form, it can be stale, uninspired, and failing to act.

This manifests as feeling stuck and restless. Feelings of self-loathing and being overly emotional are common side effects of stagnant water.

To remedy an excess of water, work with fire or earth. Be in the here and now. Learn how to protect yourself psychically.

To increase your inner water, immerse yourself in water! Place salt in your bath to cleanse old energy or practice misogi (Shinto purification ritual). You could also work with the cycles of the moon.

The angels of the West Waters are Archangel Raphael and Archeia Mary. They govern the angels of healing. Call them in to bring harmony to your mind, body, and soul.

THE ACE OF CUPS

GENERAL READING

In general, the Ace of Cups is a beautiful card to draw and is considered one of the best cards to receive in a love reading. This card ushers in a time of new beginnings for which you feel incredibly blessed. You have a renewed sense of hope. Happy news has restored your faith. You are optimistic and looking forward to the unfolding of your future.

WORK READING

In work circumstances, the Ace of Cups can herald a new job. If this is the case, you have made a great choice and will be very contented in your new workplace.

It is becoming increasingly important that your career choice brings you a sense of fulfilment. You can no longer "do it for the money." Your soul is longing for you to tap into your destined life purpose. It's time you share your magic with the world.

LOVE READING

In love readings, the Ace of Cups indicates happy times. Perhaps you have recently met someone wonderful, and romantic feelings are stirring your heart. This is the card of true love, so know that your feelings for one another are the real deal.

If you are already in an established relationship, you are entering a period where you feel very close. Your love runs deep.

When single, this card says open your heart to love! Wear your heart on your sleeve.

This card can indicate news of an engagement, wedding, pregnancy, or renewal of vows.

FINANCIAL READING

From a financial viewpoint, the Ace of Cups is a positive card. You feel grateful for all you have, and in return, the Universe responds to your energy and continues providing. This is a time of plenty. Share your wealth; there is more than enough to go around.

This card may indicate that you are purchasing a lovely new home. Look out for the Four of Wands to clarify this.

SPIRITUALITY READING

Spiritually speaking, the Ace of Cups says you are in the flow. This is an amazing time when you feel in touch with your soul. Synchronicities and blessings are unfolding all around you. There is a sense of reciprocity; the Universe keeps giving you gifts, and naturally, you extend generosity towards others.

You may be a healer or psychic reader. You have a connection to the Divine. Share this gift with others.

WELL-BEING READING

Well-being related, the Ace of Cups brings you healing and miracles. Any previous health challenges are now being ironed out. Wellness is increasing day by day, leaving you in high spirits. You take responsibility for your own peace and have a high level of emotional intelligence. You are focussing on yourself. Continue cultivating self-love. Acceptance and forgiveness serve you well.

ASSOCIATED KEYPHRASES
A pregnancy
A new home
Falling in love
Happiness
Good news
Emotional fulfilment
Forgiveness
Healing

THE TWO OF CUPS

GENERAL READING

In general, the Two of Cups is a lovely card to draw. It often appears in love readings and represents harmony. However, its beautiful meaning extends to all relationships in our lives, whether that be friendships or even business partnerships. This card signifies that things are going well. There is mutual respect between parties. You feel understood and supported by others. You can trust the intentions of those close to you.

WORK READING

In work circumstances, the Two of Cups indicates that a job application will be successful. This move suits you down to the ground, with a position that is a great fit.

If you are not looking elsewhere, this card suggests you are well-supported within your workplace. You and your peers have a common goal: to triumph. The key to success is seen in combining everyone's strengths, and there is a notable atmosphere of collaboration and cooperation among the team. The energy surrounding your career path is positive.

LOVE READING

In love readings, the Two of Cups is one of the best cards you can draw, for this is the card of true love. You may be entering into a new relationship, and if so, there is a strong connection. This person's energy feels so familiar to you. It's as though you already know each other. The attraction you feel is mutual. You both have good intentions for this relationship.

If you are in a long-term relationship, you have a solid partnership that you can trust. You and your partner are on the same page and want the same things. You are very compatible. This union will stand the test of time.

This card can indicate marriage if you are asking where a relationship will lead. If you are asking about an estranged lover who will return, this card says yes, they will.

FINANCIAL READING

From a financial viewpoint, the Two of Cups can indicate a joint purchase. Perhaps you are considering buying a home or investing in a business with someone. This would be a fruitful venture and a great candidate to share your journey with.

This card sometimes represents hiring a life coach, an assistant, a financial advisor, or even embarking upon a new training course. Someone in your life can teach you about money and how to make more of it.

SPIRITUALITY READING

Spiritually speaking, the Two of Cups reminds you that you are never alone. Your spirit guides, angels, and ancestors are now drawing near to offer you support. If you have been feeling fragmented, use breathwork to ground your energy back towards yourself. You can come back into alignment by focusing on the present moment. Work on integrating your yin and yang energies to attain harmony.

You will feel a deep connection to any new people that currently enter your life as if you are kindred spirits. Know that they have been divinely directed to cross your path for mutual benefit.

WELL-BEING READING

Well-being related, the Two of Cups indicates that you are healing. You have accepted your past and mended your wounds. Now, you are enjoying the contented feelings of harmony that come with acceptance. You can help others by sharing how you overcome your challenges. It's a good time to offer your healing wisdom.

This card reminds you to keep company. Being with others serves you well.

ASSOCIATED KEYPHRASES
A romantic connection
A balanced partnership
A resolution is reached
Compromise serves you well
Forgiveness brings you peace
Mutual respect for others
Make a commitment
Working together

THE THREE OF CUPS

GENERAL READING

In general, drawing the Three of Cups is a very positive omen. It indicates that there is (or soon will be) a reason to celebrate. This is the card of fertility, friendship, and fun-filled gatherings. Happy memories are about to be made or good news revealed. Cheers to that!

WORK READING

In work circumstances, the Three of Cups is a fabulous card that signifies good news. If you are currently working, remember that teamwork makes the dream work. Coming together with your plans will create an even better outcome than if you go at it alone.

People around you notice your talents and want to be around your high vibrational energy. If you are considering applying for a new position, then absolutely go for it! You will be successful.

LOVE READING

In love readings, the Three of Cups has several interpretations, so check surrounding cards for clarity. It is the friendship card, and its arrival can indicate just that. Good company and friends are all you need at this moment in time. Trust your circle, spend time with them, and let your hair down. Laughter is medicine.

If you are in a relationship, this card can mean that you and your lover are best friends, which is truly wonderful. Lucky you! Yet, it can also mean that a relationship has become platonic and needs spicing up.

This is also one of the pregnancy cards. If you are trying to conceive, this is a good sign that you could be celebrating very soon.

Finally, if you are doubting the loyalty of your partner (for good reason), then trust your suspicions. This card can indicate a love triangle. But, before your alarm bells go ringing, seek out clarifying cards. Remember that this card alone in an upright position is highly positive. The Devil, the Seven of Swords, or the High Priestess make combinations of concern.

FINANCIAL READING

From a financial viewpoint, the Three of Cups indicates that your money situation could be about to improve, especially if this card is in relation to a new career opportunity. This is a great time to treat yourself. You deserve recognition and rewards for your achievements. Just be careful not to splash out too much. With all the excitement in the air, this is a time when you may overindulge or overspend.

SPIRITUALITY READING

Spiritually speaking, the Three of Cups says that you are counting your blessings. Your positive thoughts are planting energetic seeds into the Universe; rewards will reap in the future. Your spiritual guides and guardian angels gather around you, ready to offer sound guidance. Remember to invite them into your life situations.

WELL-BEING READING

Well-being related, the Three of Cups indicates that you should see an improvement in your mood and thus in your vitality. Your spirits are high, and this will manifest as happiness and contentment. If you have been unwell, recovery is on the horizon.

This card can sometimes represent an alcoholic.

ASSOCIATED KEYPHRASES
Surround yourself with friends
A celebration
Fertility
A happy occasion
Good news
A "well done" is on its way
Getting what you wanted
People are happy for you

THE FOUR OF CUPS

GENERAL READING

In general, the Four of Cups arises when you feel that what is being offered is simply not enough. It may seem as though something you once wanted has lost its sparkle. However, it's likely that you have not been making time for yourself, and now life just seems like one big grind. There is a sense of boredom and lack of lustre for life. It's time to reconnect to your soul.

WORK READING

In work circumstances, the Four of Cups arises when you desperately need a career change or break. Your work tasks may feel tedious and unfulfilling. You are only plodding on for the sake of the money.

You are being reminded that you have the power to bring positive changes to your life. Don't bury your head in the sand any longer. Look for a new job. You need a challenge to stimulate and inspire you.

LOVE READING

In love readings, the Four of Cups indicates that a relationship has lost its zing. Before you think the grass is greener, make sure you have made an effort within your existing relationship. Often, the dissatisfaction we associate with a partner is a projection of our boredom with life. See if you can revive this relationship with fun before you throw the towel in.

If you are single, you may feel fed up with waiting for love to arrive. Perhaps you have given up on the prospect of having a partner, which prevents you from seeing people in a sexual way. Energetically, this belief shuts you down from attracting romance. Try a change in perspective.

FINANCIAL READING

From a financial viewpoint, the Four of Cups is not a great card. Although it doesn't indicate money loss, it does suggest that you are not financially satisfied. If you are selling a home, for example, you may be struggling to get the total value of your property.

In work, you may feel stagnant. Perhaps you are not achieving the necessary figures or sales. You are feeling disenchanted, but this card assures you there is a way out! You just can't see it yet. Someone else's point of view will help you. Remember to keep an open mind.

SPIRITUALITY READING

Spiritually speaking, the Four of Cups has you feeling blocked. Not following your heart has caused stagnation within you. You have been spending too much time focussing on a particular area of your life and neglected the whispers from your soul. This imbalance can easily be remedied by connecting to Source energy.

Remember, your garden grows where you water it.

WELL-BEING READING

Well-being related, the Four of Cups urges you to go within. If you are feeling isolated, arrange a date with a friend. You may feel like you can't be bothered now, but if you make the effort, you will enjoy the benefits and be glad you did so. Both your mood and energy could be low.

Don't compare your life to others. Instead, make a list of what is working well in your life to lighten yourself up. Try a therapy such as acupuncture to get your chi flowing.

ASSOCIATED KEYPHRASES
Boredom
Dissatisfaction
Apathy
Not seeing opportunities right in front of you
Feeling stuck
A situation didn't live up to your expectations
Unwilling to look at your circumstances
Fed up

THE FIVE OF CUPS

GENERAL READING

In general, the Five of Cups talks about disappointment. Something didn't work out as you had hoped. Rather than dwell on the negative, seek help and support to get out of this mindset. It's time to forgive yourself (or others) and move on. There is the feeling that all is lost when this card appears, yet that is an illusion. The two standing cups show us something remains. If only it could be seen.

WORK READING

In work circumstances, the Five of Cups suggests that you may feel like you have made a mess of something. You cannot backtrack from what has occurred, so you must learn to accept your reality. Could it be that you are being too hard on yourself? Are things as bad as you're perceiving? You may feel like abandoning a project or your workplace. Let your emotions settle before you make big changes.

If you are asking if you should move to a new place of work or embark upon a new project, this card says no, as you will later regret it.

LOVE READING

In love readings, the Five of Cups is a bitter card to draw. You may be feeling abandoned or alone. If you are going through a breakup, you know in your heart that this is for your best, yet it doesn't take away those feelings of grief. You will get back on your feet in time.

If you are thinking of straying from your partner, this card promises you will get caught cheating and regret it. Don't go there.

If you are single and not ready to mingle, you are likely hung up on the past. Try to move on. You deserve peace.

FINANCIAL READING

From a financial viewpoint, the Five of Cups denotes losses. Please don't take your chances and gamble right now. Avoid making significant purchases, or you may come to regret it. If you are looking for a new house or car, wait. Things are not what they seem. Problems will arise, and you will wish you never got involved. Something may be more trouble than it's worth, so hold off for now.

Finally, don't loan out money. You won't get it back.

SPIRITUALITY READING

Spiritually speaking, the Five of Cups sees a dark cloud over you. Life has been hard and unfair, but your spiritual team has never left your side. They are urging you to come back into the light. Like the man in the card, you, too, should shield your energy. Nay-sayers and psychic vampires are feeding off what little energy you have left. Cloak yourself up in the light of your guides and rest.

WELL-BEING READING

Well-being related, the Five of Cups draws attention to your mental and emotional well-being. Sometimes, this card can indicate that alcohol is affecting your life or the pain of being the child of an alcoholic parent is still causing issues in your present.

You need a change in perception to lift your negative mindset. If you are emotionally unstable and feel like you are battling mental illness, seek professional help to navigate through your problems.

ASSOCIATED KEYPHRASES
Loss
Regret
Disappointment
Fearing the worst
Cup-is-half-empty attitude
Dwelling on the past
Sadness
Self-pity

THE SIX OF CUPS

GENERAL READING

In general, the Six of Cups signifies that someone from the past is coming forward. This can be anyone, from an old school friend to an estranged family member or even a past lover. Perhaps there will be a reunion, and you will have the opportunity to reminisce. This is the card of fond memories.

Sometimes, this card can reflect your children (if you have them) or your inner child.

WORK READING

In work circumstances, the Six of Cups may represent working with children or families. If you have drawn this card in relation to your job, then you probably have a long history within your workplace. There is a pleasant atmosphere, and your colleagues feel almost like family. You feel supported and cared for.

If you feel stuck within your work choice, then take time to relive your childhood passions. Persuing activities that bring you joy may lead you to your destined career path.

LOVE READING

In love readings, the Six of Cups is a beautiful card to draw. It can represent childhood sweethearts and kindred spirits.

If you are in a relationship, you're likely to have a very close bond with your other half. There is lots of tenderness and care.

If you are just striking up a relationship with someone, it may feel like you have finally met your match. This connection may feel intense as if you have known each other before. Maybe this is so! After all, this is one of the soul mate cards.

If you are single, this card can mean that you are going to settle with someone you already know, someone from your past.

If you are asking how someone feels about you, this card can indicate that your interest just wants to be friends. Check surrounding cards for clarity.

FINANCIAL READING

From a Financial viewpoint, the Six of Cups has you feeling generous. You are contented within yourself and inspired to share your wealth, knowledge, or time.

Investments that you have made are stable and long-lasting. Whether it's in education or a physical investment, it is safe to spend on things for your future.

Sometimes, this card can indicate that you are about to inherit some abundance. Look for other wealth cards to support this interpretation.

SPIRITUALITY READING

Spiritually speaking, the Six of Cups brings you freedom and joy. This is a wonderful period in which you can take off the mask and be yourself.

Allow yourself to tap into your inner child and see the world through the eyes of magick.

People who are involved in your life at present are karmically linked to you. Meditate or try hypnotherapy to understand the spiritual lessons unfolding for you.

WELL-BEING READING

Well-being related, the Six of Cups has you feeling contented. Your emotional well-being is good. Continue focusing on happy memories to maintain this state of being carefree.

Look to your past for the answers to any health issues you may have. You cannot change things, but you will be able to track key events or turning points and thus implement improvements for the future.

ASSOCIATED KEYPHRASES
Sentimental
Nostalgic
Helpful people
Kindness
Reunions
A happy childhood
Making happy memories
Children

THE SEVEN OF CUPS

GENERAL READING

In general, the Seven of Cups comes in when you have too many options before you. Perhaps you are living in a bit of a fantasy world and need to face reality. Ideas are plenty, but it seems that while you are busy dreaming, you are not engaged in doing!

Being stuck in your head will cause you mental burnout. It's time to make a decision and stick to it for your own sanity.

WORK READING

In work circumstances, the Seven of Cups suggests that you are spreading yourself thin. By trying to do too much, you are lowering the standard of your work. Perhaps you are failing to complete projects because you are flitting from one brilliant idea to the next. Make a to-do list of priorities and start to work through it.

You may feel like you need a total change in work status but find yourself immobilised when implementing the necessary steps.

LOVE READING

In love readings, the Seven of Cups may have you infatuated. If you are indecisive about someone, take that as a red flag. Trust your gut instincts. Remember that actions speak louder than words.

If you have multiple options and are confused, remember that not all that glitters is gold. Take your time when making decisions, and don't be swayed by appearances. If something seems too good to be true, it likely is.

FINANCIAL READING

From a financial viewpoint, the Seven of Cups asks you to be honest. Look at the facts and figures. Quick-fix loans and investment schemes can send you down a slippery slope of debt.

Rather than looking for ways to get rich quick, think about how you can make things last. You are feeling overstretched, so cut back and be realistic. Think about tomorrow.

SPIRITUALITY READING

Spiritually speaking, the Seven of Cups says that you need grounding! Perhaps you have been delving into your spiritual side a bit too much and are feeling way out there! Come back to Earth.

This card can also suggest that your energy is scattered. Try being in the present moment to bring balance back to your life.

WELL-BEING READING

Well-being related, the Seven of Cups can indicate you feel overwhelmed. Your thoughts may be running away with you, causing unrest and anxiety. Share your concerns with an appropriate healthcare provider. External support will help you get a grip on things and set you on the right footing.

This card can indicate a health condition under investigation.

ASSOCIATED KEYPHRASES
So many choices!
Indecision
Fantasies
Unrealistic expectations
ADHD
Temptation
Confusion
Make a decision!

THE EIGHT OF CUPS

GENERAL READING

In general, the Eight of Cups offers you the chance to make major adjustments in your life. Often, these changes are unwanted and can be forced upon you, so naturally, feelings of fear or sadness can accompany this card. It's time to move on and heal. Explore unchartered territories to bring joy back into your life.

WORK READING

In work circumstances, the Eight of Cups can indicate a job loss. You may have been fired, made redundant, or perhaps you are walking away because your role is no longer providing emotional satisfaction. Despite this being a difficult position, trust that you are on the right path. Set the bar higher; you deserve more.

As a career, this card can represent someone who helps people to overcome their emotional difficulties or addictions. That could be a therapist or anyone who helps others to change their perception.

LOVE READING

In love readings, the Eight of Cups indicates sadness and unfulfillment. You may feel lonely; perhaps you are thinking of leaving your relationship. You're not sure how much more you can take. It's time to move on.

Or maybe you have just come out of a relationship, and you are the one who is feeling abandoned. You may feel as though you won't get over this person now, but you will in time.

Remember that other people cannot complete you. If you feel something is missing from your life, it's time to look within.

FINANCIAL READING

From a financial viewpoint, the Eight of Cups could indicate that it's time to let go of investments that are not working. For example, if your car constantly needs repairs, this card is a sign to cut your losses.

Review your finances and clear away any unnecessary drains on your funds. Cancel subscriptions you no longer use. If other people are sapping your hard-earned money, it's time to be brave and say no!

This is not a good time to buy.

SPIRITUALITY READING

Spiritually speaking, the Eight of Cups is a powerful card to draw. This is a wake-up call from your soul. Perhaps a crisis has brought you to question the meaning of your life. The teachings of this card can be loud to get your attention. It often arises when you have failed to implement change, and now that choice has been taken from you. Spiritually, you are longing for something deep. You may be unsure of what you are even seeking; listen to the whispers of your soul. Look out for synchronicity to lead the way.

WELL-BEING READING

Well-being related, the Eight of Cups suggests that you are struggling with your emotional health. You may be feeling lost and hopeless. At its worst, it signifies depression and even not wanting to be here anymore. Seek immediate help if this is how you feel.

Additionally, this card can denote someone trying to walk away from their addictions. It's an arduous journey, but you must keep on going.

If you have been unsuccessful in receiving a diagnosis or suitable treatment plan, keep searching. Don't settle for less. There are answers to be found.

ASSOCIATED KEYPHRASES
Looking for something better
Turning your back on someone
Abandoning a project
The dark night of the soul
Moving on
Depression
Withdrawing
Walk away, you won't look back.

THE NINE OF CUPS

GENERAL READING

In general, the Nine of Cups is a wonderful card to draw. It is well known (along with the Star) as the wish card. When it arrives in your reading, know that a wonderful blessing is about to unfold in your life. What you have been wanting is finally about to manifest. This happy result will have you feeling very pleased with yourself indeed. Your heart is full and contented.

WORK READING

In work circumstances, the Nine of Cups brings you positive news. You have done a good job, and you know it. There could be a celebration, pay raise, or recognition in the air. There will be a happy change at work.

If you have recently applied for a job, this card indicates that you will get what you most want. You will be successful. Congratulations.

LOVE READING

In love readings, the Nine of Cups represents all the good feelings. You have entered a lucky period, and everything seems to be going your way. Relationships are shifting into a happier stage, and you feel a deep appreciation towards your partner.

If you are single and have a love interest, this card indicates that you will get to go on a date together. How exciting!

FINANCIAL READING

From a financial viewpoint, the Nine of Cups brings you abundance! This is a blissful time when all your needs are met. You have accomplished your goals, and things turned out even better than you expected. Put your feet up and enjoy the fruits of your labour.

SPIRITUALITY READING

Spiritually speaking, the Nine of Cups arrives when you learn to enjoy the journey, not just the destination. You feel very humble for your gifts and want to share your bounty with others. You are deeply connected to the wisdom of your soul, and the material wealth you have acquired is simply the icing on the cake and not the source of your happiness. Your higher heart is awakened. You feel blessed.

WELL-BEING READING

Well-being related, the Nine of Cups indicates a time of deep joy and contentment. Your health and well-being are in great shape. Emotionally, you feel like the cat that got the cream. All is well.

Any illness should soon be a thing of the past.

ASSOCIATED KEYPHRASES
Your dreams come true
Deep satisfaction
Indulgence

Feeling grateful
Happiness
Success
Make a wish
You will get what you want

THE TEN OF CUPS

GENERAL READING

In general, the Ten of Cups is the card of love and harmony. You are well supported by your family or circle and feel a deep sense of belonging. It feels so good to love and appreciate others and to feel cherished back in return. Your home is filled with happiness. You have something money cannot buy, and you wouldn't swap it for the world. Life is good. Shared blessings are coming your way.

WORK READING

In work circumstances, the Ten of Cups brings you a sense of community. You gel well with your colleagues; they've got your back as you have theirs. You love your job; it brings you deep satisfaction and contentment. You feel at home with your career.

If you are asking about a new job, take this card as a positive sign. You will fit in well at your new place of work. This is a successful time.

This card can indicate working from home or being a stay-at-home parent.

LOVE READING

In love readings, the Ten of Cups is a beautiful card to draw as it signifies true love. The feelings that you have for your partner are mutual. You make a great team, working together as a unified front. By investing in each other with love and care, you have built a solid future you can trust. Your emotional needs are met. There is so much happiness at home.

If you are asking about the outcome of a relationship, this card signifies a lasting relationship, setting up a home together, and even marriage and children.

FINANCIAL READING

From a financial viewpoint, the Ten of Cups indicates that you are financially stable. You have looked after your purse strings very well, and anywhere you have invested is safe. Although, you are more interested in attaining happiness rather than making money. When your relationships are working well, you feel emotionally rich. With your positive attitude and attentiveness, you really can have it all.

This card can indicate purchasing a new home. Go ahead; you will find peace there.

SPIRITUALITY READING

Spiritually speaking, the Ten of Cups arrives when you are feeling spiritually connected. You have found your place in the world, and this is a blissful state of awareness to achieve. You will likely be noticing signs from your spiritual team—perhaps a white feather or a rainbow, just like in the card. You're on the right path. Keep up the good work.

WELL-BEING READING

Well-being related, the Ten of Cups indicates that your heart is full. Life is unfolding in a beautiful way, and you feel incredibly grateful to be here. This is a wonderful time for you and your loved ones. If you are feeling broody, a new addition to the family would be the icing on the cake.

Your sense of wellness is increasing.

ASSOCIATED KEYPHRASES
A wish fulfilled
Emotional bliss
Happy family
Contentment
A happy ending
A silver lining
Feeling loved
Good news

COURT CARDS:
THE CUPS ARCHETYPES

The following cards represent the archetypal personalities of the court cards in the suit of cups.

The cups or water court cards mainly represent the personality that the querent is expressing or needs to align with to achieve their goal.

Cups sometimes (not always) represent the star signs Scorpio, Pisces, and Cancer.

Cups people are sensitive, emotional, and intuitive. They can represent family members, loved ones, and healers. They can speak for a wide range of feelings.

These cards often arise when you are focused on increasing happiness and caring about family or loved ones.

PAGE of CUPS.

THE PAGE OF CUPS

GENERAL READING

In general, the Page of Cups can indicate that happy news or an invitation is on the horizon. Maybe you will be successful with a job interview or hear news of a family pregnancy. Perhaps you will unexpectedly be asked out on a date. Whatever the offer, know that it will stir your emotions in a positive way.

This card often represents sensitive or creative children in our lives.

WORK READING

In work circumstances, the Page of Cups could well be offering you satisfying news in terms of work! This is usually a subtle change that makes a big difference to the quality of your experience.

This card can represent someone who is artistic and creative. A job that feels like a hobby would suit your carefree personality. Sometimes, you may need a rocket up your backside as your dreamy imagination can take over and lead to procrastination.

LOVE READING

In love readings, the Page of Cups indicates that your love interest is curious about you. They want to get to know you deeper. Usually, this card suggests that you will be asked out for a date, but don't sit about daydreaming and wait for it to happen. Be proactive! Make it obvious that you are interested, as sometimes this card can represent someone who finds it difficult to express their feelings. Don't take things too seriously.

This card pull indicates that you have romantic admirers.

FINANCIAL READING

From a financial viewpoint, the Page of Cups asks you to be sensible! You may feel sentimental and want to spoil those you love but remember that you cannot buy others' affection. This is a time when you are emotionally sensitive, and people or causes may be pulling on your heartstrings. Use your head, not your heart, when dealing with finances.

SPIRITUALITY READING

Spiritually speaking, the Page of Cups offers you an invitation from your higher self. The higher consciousness within you is beckoning to become acquainted. Your psychic senses are stirring. You may experience powerful visions or hear a subtle voice guiding you forward. Trust in yourself! You are psychically awakening.

WELL-BEING READING

Well-being related the Page of Cups asks you to address inner child issues. If you are feeling triggered by other people, then it's time to ask yourself why they are disturbing your peace. What unhealed emotions within you are being stirred? If you are feeling irritable, be mindful of being childish. Take a nap; have some time to yourself. Ensure your basic needs are being met to keep your emotions balanced.

ASSOCIATED KEYPHRASES

A date
Feeling inspired
Creative
Artistic
Intuitive
A surprise invitation
Pleasant news
An admirer

THE KNIGHT OF CUPS

GENERAL READING

In general, the Knight of Cups is a lovely card to draw. It arrives in your spread when you are on a personal quest for happiness, but there is no rush. You are enjoying the journey, dreaming up your days as you go by. You are happy-go-lucky and tend to bring the best out in people.

This is also a card of sexual attraction. If you are wondering about pursuing someone, this card tells you to go for it! Wear your heart on your sleeve.

WORK READING

In work circumstances, the Knight of Cups asks you to follow your heart. By simply being yourself and serving as an inspiration, you are a gentle leader who motivates the workforce to step up and perform at their best.

Your ideas have a romantic tone and captivating effect on people's minds due to your passion and enthusiasm. Don't be surprised if you are headhunted by an organisation, for your attention to detail is second to none.

This card can represent someone who has a creative job or an incoming offer. Put yourself out there.

LOVE READING

In love readings, the Knight of Cups is a great card to draw. After all, he is Mr. Lover Lover.

What is being offered romantically is genuine. This is a love that you can trust. Whether you are the Knight of Cups or he is actively pursuing you, know that commitment is being offered.

This Knight can be very romantic and may have traditional values. Expect flowers and kind gestures. This is not a front; this is a genuinely loving person.

If you are single, expect an offer! If you are taken, perhaps your other half is planning a lovely surprise for you.

FINANCIAL READING

From a financial viewpoint, the Knight of Cups comes to lend you a hand. If you have been trying to fathom how to increase your income, seek guidance from a mentor. An opportunity might be about to come your way, but you must be strict with yourself and move with haste.

Time is of the essence, and your laid-back attitude could let this chance slip through your fingers. Take the offer!

SPIRITUALITY READING

Spiritually speaking, the Knight of Cups represents your guardian angel or spirit guide. This is a very special time when your guardians are drawing close. They offer you extra protection, courage, and wisdom. Your spiritual interests may have peaked, the holy grail of your heart beckoning for you to discover the mystical truths of your soul.

You are hungry for knowledge, but Rome wasn't built in a day. Relax, knowing that you are on the right path. Stay committed.

WELL-BEING READING

Well-being related, the Knight of Cups represents feelings of contentment. There are things that you want to manifest and goals that you strive for, but you are taking everything in your stride. Your approach to life is happy and relaxed, which greatly impacts your sense of well-being.

If you are seeking test results, answers will soon arrive. Stay optimistic and visualise the best outcome. You are in good hands.

ASSOCIATED KEYPHRASES

A romantic person
A knight in shining armour
A proposal or offer
Wanting to make a difference
Having a big heart
Infatuation
A spiritual adventure
Altruism

THE QUEEN OF CUPS

GENERAL READING

In general, the Queen of Cups represents a feminine aspect of yourself or a woman in your life. She can be your mother, wife, or even a loyal friend. This queen is the most nurturing of all and will mother you with tenderness. Being a water sign makes her naturally intuitive and in touch with her emotions.

Drawing this card indicates that you are attentive to those who are important in your life. You are generous and loving. Keep giving your energy to a worthwhile cause and see how your proverbial garden grows.

WORK READING

In work circumstances, the Queen of Cups is a creative soul and can represent artists, writers, and healers. Perhaps you have a strong spiritual calling and are thinking of making a career out of your gifts. This card says you are very talented at what you do and will attract clients or customers easily because of your warm, caring nature.

Often, she can represent a stay-at-home mother or someone who works with children.

If you are unhappy with your job or work status, you must follow your heart. Otherwise, you will easily become bored and depressed at work.

LOVE READING

In love readings, the Queen of Cups is a wonderful card to draw. She represents feeling in love and being admired.

If you are asking how someone feels about you, this card indicates that you have stirred someone's heart. This is more than physical attraction; this person really cares for you. If you are asking about the outcome of a relationship, then this card denotes that love is in the air.

FINANCIAL READING

From a financial viewpoint, the Queen of Cups asks you to look after your investments. It would be a good idea to protect your ideas and your dreams. You tend to give of yourself freely but know that you should keep your energy for yourself for now. Don't spread yourself too thin and focus on one project at a time. There is an opportunity to grow your wealth so long as you don't allow proverbial weeds to strangle the life force out of your ideas.

Generally, you are feeling grateful and contented on a materialistic level.

SPIRITUALITY READING

Spiritually speaking, the Queen of Cups is the empath. Her appearance in your spread signifies that your psychic gifts are increasing. You feel deeply, and sometimes, you may take ownership of energies that do not belong to you. You want to help others and are a natural healer. Ensuring your energy is always protected means you will always have more to give. Shield your solar plexus centre.

WELL-BEING READING

Well-being related, the Queen of Cups is asking you to take care of yourself! Serving others for little or no reward can be your downfall. The key word here is reciprocity. If you keep giving without learning to receive, you will become exhausted or feel like a doormat. People gravitate towards you with their problems, and while this is ok from time to time, don't let others take advantage. You may need to set up some boundaries and learn to say no. Remember, you can't pour from an empty jug. Depleting yourself serves no one. Look after yourself for a change.

ASSOCIATED KEYPHRASES
Feeling emotional
Loving
Caring
Sensitive
Intuitive
A fulfilling homelife
Nurturing others
A pregnancy

THE KING OF CUPS

GENERAL READING

In general, the King of Cups represents a mature man in your life. This could be a father figure, mentor, husband, or therapist. This is someone who has vast emotional intelligence and will be able to provide you with valuable guidance and support.

If this card represents an aspect of yourself, perhaps someone is relying upon you to help them navigate life's challenges. You are well-versed in the ups and downs of life and thus have much wisdom to offer. You take people under your wing with care and compassion.

WORK READING

In work circumstances, the King of Cups is a fair leader. Drawing this card suggests that you possess extraordinary talent when it comes to expressing yourself and communicating effectively. You understand people on a deeper level than most, and so your negotiation skills are second to none. People naturally warm to you; they can sense that you genuinely care. You would make an excellent councillor, therapist, nurse, doctor, or coach. Believe in yourself and work with passion.

Perhaps a man at work has a soft spot for you!

LOVE READING

In love readings, the King of Cups represents a love you can trust. If you are in a relationship, you are likely married. Your king is fully committed to you and is someone that you can rely on. Unlike the other kings, the King of Cups is strongly in touch with his feminine side. He is intuitive and likes a good conversation.

If you are asking about the outcome of a relationship, then know that this union is stable. There could be an offer of marriage or moving in together.

If you want to know how someone feels about you, this card means they are in love. Truly, madly, deeply.

FINANCIAL READING

From a financial viewpoint, the King of Cups reminds you not to allow fluctuating finances to affect you mentally. Of course, get on top of things and face issues head-on, but don't let this give you sleepless nights.

You may not have as much wealth as you would like and may feel the burden of having to provide for your family. Give yourself credit where it's due; you can be hard on yourself.

Perhaps you need to learn to say no to financial demands from your partner or children. Generous by nature, you just love to give.

SPIRITUALITY READING

Spiritually speaking, the King of Cups says you are spiritually aware. You've had a tough life but learned to heal rather than feel like a victim. This has instilled you with a deep wisdom that others can feel. People feel safe in your presence and total strangers may open up and share their troubles and stories. Clear your energy field after such circumstances so you do not lose your vital energy.

WELL-BEING READING

Well-being related, the King of Cups denotes that you are physically strong and well. It is your emotions that you need to keep an eye on. Make time for self-care, take a swim, or walk by water to soothe your soul. This will allow you to recharge your batteries and help you to switch off from worries.

ASSOCIATED KEYPHRASES

Loyalty
Empathy
A man in touch with his emotions
A life partner
Someone who you can rely on
Wise counsel
Marriage or a proposal
A lasting commitment

THE SUIT OF SWORDS

The suit of swords is governed by the element of air. The power of air resides in the direction of the east. These cards represent situations that require a lot of thought and decision-making. They represent ideas, communication, and conflict.

Air, in its positive expression, is cleansing and refreshing. It represents mastery over the mind and aids connection to your higher self or the Divine mind. With the power of air, you can think clearly and tap into brilliant ideas. You will know exactly how to execute your plans swiftly and confidently.

When air is expressed in its negative form, it leads to confusion and feelings of being stifled and unclear. Racing thoughts and irrational decisions are made when we are unfocused. This manifests as anxiety, poor mental health, and conflict with others.

To remedy the afflictions governed by air (the mind), spend time journaling to weed out unhelpful beliefs. Work on reprogramming your subconscious mind with a therapist, a healer, or by practising meditation. Burn incense in your home and practice breathwork to connect deeper to this element.

The angels of the east are Archangel Michael and Archeia Faith. They govern the angels of truth. Call them in to bring clarity and purpose to your life.

THE ACE OF SWORDS

GENERAL READING

In general, the Ace of Swords is a brilliant card that symbolizes new beginnings. You have matured mentally, and through your change in perspective, you have now unlocked new doorways of opportunity. You are ready to embrace this fresh start. The fog has finally lifted. You know exactly what you want and are excited to implement positive change. You are about to embrace your well-deserved silver lining.

WORK READING

In work circumstances, the Ace of Swords indicates that you haven't always had it easy. Yet, past challenges have served you well. You have embraced life's lessons, which have defined who you are today.

Lately, you may find yourself feeling curious about your true life purpose. Perhaps you have even been questioning your career choice. Know that you are in alignment with the next step of your journey.

Follow this newly inspired passion. These breadcrumbs from your soul will lead you toward your ultimate work journey.

A sudden work opportunity may arise. Be sure to grab it with both hands. It's time to believe in yourself and make things happen.

LOVE READING

In love readings, the Ace of Swords is a great card to pull if you have been through a difficult relationship patch. It says that with honest communication, you can turn things around and have a fresh start. You may not have been expecting this, but a sudden sense of clarity overcomes you, and now you know what you want. Seek out a relationship counsellor or create a plan together. What positive action steps can you both take to keep on track?

If you are single and happy, then carry on! On the other hand, if you are looking for love, this card may indicate that someone not your usual type may catch your attention. Be open-minded and give them a chance. This may be a good match for you.

FINANCIAL READING

From a financial viewpoint, the Ace of Swords asks you to get real. No more unnecessary spending unless you really can afford it. This is the time to take an inventory of your finances. Be willing to look at any debts you may have accrued and come up with solutions to bring more balance to your finances. A few short-term sacrifices will go a long way.

If you are thinking of investing or making a large purchase, such as a new home, just get your thinking cap on. Weigh up the pros and cons. Don't get emotional over things. Let your head lead this time.

SPIRITUALITY READING

Spiritually speaking, the Ace of Swords ushers in a time of revelations and new understanding. Your soul has endured some challenging times, but you are far from broken. You have been forged, like the mighty sword of truth, and now is your time of resurrection. Low vibrational, false things are no longer of interest to you.

You are fully committed to slaying the ego and rising into the Divine being you came here to be.

WELL-BEING READING

Well-being related, the Ace of Swords brings you answers. If you have had any physical, emotional, or mental issues, the solutions you need are now coming to light. This could appear in the form of professional advice, having surgery, or simply educating yourself and acting upon recommended guidance.

If you want to better your life and health, now is the time to go for it. There is improvement all around if you do.

ASSOCIATED KEYPHRASES
Breakthroughs
A double-edged sword situation
Perspective
New beginnings
Brilliant ideas
A new pathway opens up
An opportunity
Effective planning

THE TWO OF SWORDS

GENERAL READING

In general, the Two of Swords arises when you have a challenging situation before you with no idea how to handle it. You may perceive two options before you, but if you look from an objective point of view, there is probably another solution waiting to be uncovered. Until you are willing to cast aside everything you think you know, the resolution evades you.

WORK READING

In work circumstances, the Two of Swords is a card of frustration. Perhaps you are not seeing eye to eye with your colleagues. Maybe you have simply had enough of your current job, but you need the money, and so you continue plodding on.

A change is as good as a rest. Book a few days off. Spend time relaxing and dreaming, and the solutions will come to you. This could just be a temporary blip, and you may come back feeling refreshed. If not, make new plans and be prepared to forge your own pathway ahead.

LOVE READING

In love readings, the Two of Swords indicates strong feelings of uncertainty have arisen within your relationship. This could be a temporary clash of opinions. You may sense that you and your partner are not on the same wavelength. Ask yourself if this relationship is worth saving. If the answer is yes, go ahead and sort out your issues. Have an honest conversation and aim to get back on track.

If you have had a change of heart, don't make any irrational decisions. Take a step back to gain clarity first.

If you don't know where you stand within a relationship, then this is an incredibly confusing time for you. You are being asked to weigh your options and take time out for yourself. Know that if someone wanted to be with you, they would.

FINANCIAL READING

From a financial viewpoint, the Two of Swords may have you concerned about how to proceed. If you are in doubt about making a purchase, just wait. There is more than meets the eye, and this is not a time to invest.

Do not ignore debt or turn a blind eye toward the health of your finances. Don't create more stress for yourself by biting off more than you can chew.

You are moving into a period where your work must align with your values. If you do not feel as though you are making a positive impact in the world, your heart and mind will not be in coherence.

SPIRITUALITY READING

Spiritually speaking, the Two of Swords draws your attention to shadow work. There is a deep sense of frustration within but know that this uncomfortable feeling is revealing clues as to what needs to be healed.

Attaining inner peace should be your priority at this time. Go within. The answers you seek await you.

Remember, it's ok not to have everything together all the time. If we are unexposed to challenges, then how would we grow?

WELL-BEING READING

Well-being related, the Two of Swords wants you to know that you are not alone. Even though you may not feel it at times, love and support are always available from the invisible realms. Spirit know that you are mentally conflicted right now. They want you to address issues that are affecting your well-being.

Meditate, seek support, and eat healthily. Learn to love yourself enough to put your needs first. Remember, this will pass. This card can represent tension headaches and eye strain.

ASSOCIATED KEYPHRASES
Stuck in a rut
A choice needs to be made
Indecisiveness
Lack of clarity
Being at loggerheads with others
Feeling torn
A stalemate
Not having all the facts

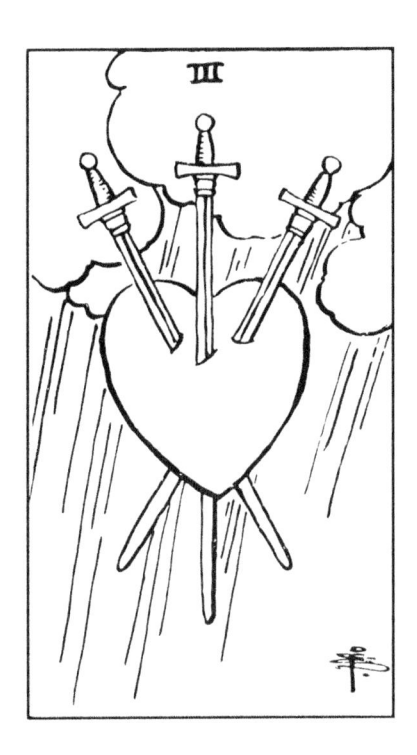

THE THREE OF SWORDS

GENERAL READING

In general, the Three of Swords is a heavy card. It represents feelings of great sadness and grief. A situation has occurred that has caused upheaval and hurt you deeply. This could signify a bereavement, the end of a relationship, or any situation that emotionally floors you.

WORK READING

In work circumstances, the Three of Swords indicates that your work is making you sad. There may be bullying at work, an inability to control your emotions, or your heart just may not be in it anymore. You must find work that makes you feel good. Put yourself out there. You deserve to be happy.

If you are unemployed and are suffering from depression, finding a sense of purpose through a career may be just what you need to bring new inspiration to your life. You will feel better if you contribute.

LOVE READING

In love readings, the Three of Swords can indicate that you have been deeply hurt within a relationship. Perhaps you are dealing with a divorce or breakup. Maybe you are still committed, yet a painful event has taken place that has left you feeling broken. Honour yourself and acknowledge your pain. Ride this out; don't put a plaster over it. Take time to heal.

If you are single, this card implies that you have your own healing journey to tend to before you move on to a new relationship. Once you have mended your heart and made peace with your past, you will be in a position to attract a relationship that is wholesome and nourishing.

FINANCIAL READING

From a financial viewpoint, the Three of Swords reminds you that you can't buy love. If someone is draining your finances, time, or energy and not giving back, it's time to ask yourself why you are tolerating this disrespectful behaviour. You are lovable and worthy. Once you understand this, you will manifest loving relationships and abundance hand-in-hand. You only attract what you think you deserve. Focus on self-love and work on your money blocks to attract more fortune.

SPIRITUALITY READING

Spiritually speaking, the Three of Swords ushers in a spiritual lesson. You are likely to find yourself in a difficult situation. But try to understand that the dark night of the soul offers you the chance for healing and positive change. There is a lesson to be uncovered, or a karmic cycle is ready to be revealed and broken.

Call in Divine support to hold you while you journey deep into your shadow aspect. True happiness is your birthright. Get through this initiation. There is light at the end of the tunnel.

WELL-BEING READING

Well-being related, the Three of Swords has you feeling unsettled. It is important to replenish your energy during this stressful period. When you are sad, you can overeat or lose your appetite entirely. You may experience a disrupted sleep pattern. However you are feeling, the key lies in allowing yourself to feel the whole spectrum of your emotions.

Embrace your sadness and soothe your inner child. Do whatever you can to raise your energy, if only slightly. Choose to eat nutritious food and rest.

This card can represent depression, poor circulation and heart issues.

ASSOCIATED KEYPHRASES
Feeling broken-hearted
Grief
Loss
Sadness
Betrayal
Depression
The end of a relationship
A revelation that hurts your heart

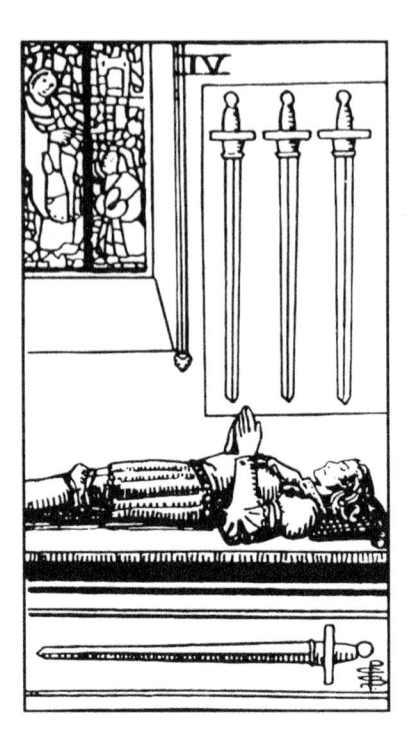

THE FOUR OF SWORDS

GENERAL READING

In general, the Four of Swords indicates that it is time to withdraw from a situation so that you can recharge and heal. You may be heading for burnout; this card frequently gives you the heads-up to slow down and replenish your energy. The idea that you must constantly strive to advance is not necessarily true. If you take a break and step away from your pursuits, things will likely be just as they were once you return.

WORK READING

In work circumstances, the Four of Swords signifies a need for change. You may feel like things are getting on top of you, but know that you cannot gain clarity amid your situation. A day off or holiday will allow you the head space to regain the strength to continue.

If you are unemployed, this card indicates that you will remain out of work for the time being. Perhaps you cannot work or are off sick or on maternity leave. Use this time to focus on yourself.

LOVE READING

In love readings, the Four of Swords asks you to put your sword down and surrender. Either you or your partner is not in the best place right now and are in desperate need of space. There is some level of emotional unavailability here. Don't take it to heart. Understand that this is a time of healing. Once clarity and recuperation have been replenished, you can aim to get your relationship on the right track.

If you are single, this card reflects feeling alone. Learn to fill your own cup. Focus on yourself for now, as you are not ready for a relationship.

FINANCIAL READING

From a financial viewpoint, the Four of Swords asks you to wait before making any big decisions. There is much thinking to do. You won't miss out by taking time off to plan your next moves.

If you are in financial difficulty, seek expert advice. Live below your means, eat in, and see where you can save short-term to get yourself back on your feet.

If you are flush, then it's time to take a well-deserved holiday. Stop working too hard, lighten up, and have some fun.

SPIRITUALITY READING

Spiritually speaking, the Four of Swords is calling you to go within. Perhaps you have lost the harmonious balance in your life. And this will leave you feeling drained and maybe a little lost.

Your soul is calling you home. Your meditation practice is overdue. Book that retreat you have been longing for, or take the desired yoga class. Listen to and follow your inspiration. Deep nourishment awaits you.

WELL-BEING READING

Well-being related, the Four of Swords reminds you of the value of being at peace. It's time to jump off the hamster wheel. This is not the time to push yourself to work harder. It is time to rest and reflect. If you keep on burning the candles at both ends, you will run yourself down into the ground. This card can indicate a visit to the hospital or a place of healing.

ASSOCIATED KEYPHRASES
Rest
Recovery
Time to reflect
Withdraw
Rejuvenation
Stop
A hospital visit/rehab
Gather your strength

THE FIVE OF SWORDS

GENERAL READING

In general, the Five of Swords indicates that conflict could be on the horizon. Some things in life are fated and unavoidable, yet this is one of the few cards that can be seen as a gentle heads-up that how you respond to a situation can heavily influence the outcome. Therefore, if you take the message of this card on board and can control your emotions (or tongue!), it is likely that you can avoid conflict altogether. Choose your battles wisely.

WORK READING

In work circumstances, the Five of Swords can indicate competition around you. Remember that jealousy is inadvertently a compliment. That green-eyed person subconsciously fears that you are better or more competent than them. Try to perceive them with compassion. After all, you are dealing with their wounded inner child.

Do not entertain gossip; it might just blow up in your face! Keep yourself to yourself, and the energies of this edgy period will blow over within no time.

LOVE READING

In love readings, the Five of Swords suggests that tension could be in the air! Have you been swallowing your words? Is a well-rehearsed mental scenario about to erupt from you at any given moment? Is the proverbial straw about to break the camel's back?

It is time to be honest if something is not sitting right with you, but please choose your timing well and make this constructive! If something is bothering you, have that difficult conversation when you feel calm. This way, your other half is more likely to take on board what you have to say. If you attack, others will defend.

Compromise can be made by both listening to each other. If pent-up anger is released in an argument, there will be no resolution, only silly tit-for-tat squabbles.

FINANCIAL READING

From a financial viewpoint, the Five of Swords asks you to hold on to your money. This is not the time to invest. Watch out for con artists, and don't be duped into lending other people money; they only have their own interests at heart and may never repay you.

If you are conflicted over finances, take a breather. The pathway ahead may not be clear at present. However, things will speed up, and you will soon turn a corner. Be patient.

SPIRITUALITY READING

Spiritually speaking, the Five of Swords arrives with the message that it is time for a check-in with your soul. Swords represent your thoughts, so this card suggests that your thinking may be a bit scatty at the moment. Remember that your energy follows your thoughts, so if you feel fragmented, retrace your thinking, and take back your energy from whatever has been draining you.

WELL-BEING READING

Well-being related, the Five of Swords reminds you to rest! You can easily overdo it when this card shows up. Perhaps you are too busy helping others when, in truth, you could do with a little support yourself. Meditation will bring peace to a busy mind.

Don't give too much of yourself away right now. Look at any situations where you are giving and not seeing a return. It may be time for a clear-out to get your energy flowing vibrantly once again.

ASSOCIATED KEYPHRASES

Don't rise to the bait
Don't get involved in other people's dramas
Think before you speak
Miscommunication
Fighting is a waste of energy
Withdraw
A person plays mind games
Gossip

THE SIX OF SWORDS

GENERAL READING

In general, the Six of Swords indicates movement and travel. If you are about to take a trip or holiday, this card assures you that you will have a wonderful time and return feeling revitalised and refreshed. If you have no travel plans, the message of this card is to be taken towards proverbial travel, as in one's life journey.

Its arrival in a spread suggests you are about to turn a corner. Try not to cling to what was. Going with the flow will ensure you land exactly where you are meant to be.

If you have just been through a difficult patch, this card is welcomed, for it foresees healing and a bright future. Even if you cannot see a clearly defined pathway, trust that the worst is now over, and you are sailing into calmer waters.

WORK READING

In work circumstances, the Six of Swords can indicate adjustments being made. Whether big or small, you can expect changes. While you may feel resistant towards these alterations, know that they are for the best in the long term. There is a hidden blessing that you will later understand.

If you have had enough at your current place of work, try something new. If you are only working to pay your bills and feel you have a deeper purpose in your career, begin to explore your interests. What do you feel drawn to?

If you are unemployed and looking for work, your current circumstance may seem bleak, but try to summon some hope. This card promises a happy change on the horizon.

LOVE READING

In love readings, the Six of Swords says that if you are in a relationship right now, you may feel as though you don't know where you stand. You may even feel like throwing in the towel and moving in a new direction but remember that the grass is not always greener. It's important to take everything into consideration and sit back and observe. Don't rush into making big decisions, especially when experiencing unsteady emotions.

If you are single, then you are being gently reminded to be more open and willing to trust new people who enter your life. Try not to compare them to people who have hurt you.

FINANCIAL READING

From a financial viewpoint, the Six of Swords has the same theme through every circumstance – uncertainty and the inability to see with great depth and clarity. Balance giving with receiving. Play it safe to avoid money slipping through your fingers, yet at the same time, be generous and use the law of attraction to manifest blessings of abundance. To do this, you must give from the heart and not out of obligation.

SPIRITUALITY READING

Spiritually speaking, the Six of Swords is a very powerful card. You have just experienced some sort of spiritual death or dark night of the soul, where you have been tested on every level. You are being called to acknowledge and celebrate your victories; you are now through the worst of your challenges. See this as a rite of passage.

Try to find the deeper meaning of your spiritual lesson to avoid repeating the cycle.

Remember that rebirth can be a painful time. It's normal to feel wounded, uncertain, and even disconnected at times, but rest assured you will come out of this with more insight and wisdom. Your life is about to become more meaningful.

WELL-BEING READING

Well-being related, the Six of Swords can indicate an emotional time. If you have had a bit of a wobble, trust that you will soon feel more stable. Can you make some space in your life to get clearer on what you wish to experience next?

Nurture yourself, take a break, visit family, and do everything you have been putting off. This will give you a small sense of accomplishment and help to centre any fragmented energy. Move your body and drink plenty of water. All things pass.

This card can signify a person with water retention, someone who is unable to let go of their emotions.

ASSOCIATED KEYPHRASES
Going on a journey
Leave the past behind
Troubles coming to an end
Happiness is around the corner
An emotional time
A change is as good as a rest
Let go
Things can only get better, even if you can't see it now

THE SEVEN OF SWORDS

GENERAL READING

In general, the Seven of Swords denotes lies and deception. This card can represent that the querent themself is up to no good. Perhaps they have been stealing, cheating, or even lying to themselves. Yet, more often than not, this card stands for someone who is about to take advantage of you and snatch something that doesn't belong to them.

When this card emerges, my advice is to be vigilant regarding your security and not get involved in anything that can trip you up.

WORK READING

In work circumstances, the Seven of Swords reminds you that there are no shortcuts up the career ladder. If you cut corners and rush, your lack of effort will be noticed. This card can sometimes indicate that a colleague is trying to take credit for your work or even take your place! Be aware. People may not be as genuine as they seem.

LOVE READING

In love readings, the Seven of Swords is seen as a red flag. At best, it can represent not knowing where you stand, having severe trust issues, or hiding skeletons in the closet. At worst, it denotes secretive behaviour, deception, or cheating. Look for the Devil, the Three of Cups, the Knight of Wands, or the Lovers for further evidence of an affair. Remember not to assume that this card always indicates an affair.

Placed with the Five of Pentacles, it could indicate a partner has lost some money and is too scared to tell you. Placed with the Fool, it could indicate a partner has been gambling. Paired with the Ace of Cups can reveal an alcoholic. Always carefully examine surrounding cards.

FINANCIAL READING

From a financial viewpoint, the Seven of Swords card is a big no-no. If someone wants you to lend them cash, know that you won't get it back. If you are petty pilfering in the office, you will get caught. If you are about to buy a new car, it might just be about to blow its engine. Keep hold of your cash at this time.

Also, be aware that this card can indicate a loss by theft. Be vigilant, lock your windows, and don't leave things lying around.

SPIRITUALITY READING

Spiritually speaking, the Seven of Swords reminds you that everything is subjected to the law of cause and effect. Should anyone unfairly take from you, know they only steal from themselves. Don't feel the need to punish people. Karma will see that the scales rebalance.

Perhaps you have been triggered into recalling a time when you felt like a victim. Take back your power. Leave the past behind you.

WELL-BEING READING

Well-being related, the Seven of Swords asks you to be honest with yourself. Are you ignoring warning signs from your body? You have reached a point where you cannot brush things under the carpet. It's time to learn to love yourself and do whatever you need to ensure good health and well-being. If you don't take this seriously now, you may later regret it when something you could have handled alone needs professional assistance. If you are already under medical care and you are not satisfied seek a second opinion.

In terms of health, this card can indicate a trip, fall or small illness such as food poisoning.

ASSOCIATED KEYPHRASES
Deception
Theft
Trickery
A liar
Denial
A secret is revealed
Do not trust face value
Gossip/defamation

THE EIGHT OF SWORDS

GENERAL READING

In general, the Eight of Swords arises when you are feeling anxious or restricted. You are in an uncomfortable position and are uncertain as to how you can free yourself. More often than not, there is an obvious way to proceed, but fears or obligations keep you stuck in a rut.

WORK READING

In work circumstances, the Eight of Swords is a positive sign that if you are unemployed and asking if you will "get the job," you will soon become bound by contract.

If you are in a position of employment already, perhaps you are itching for something new. Peers may be piling on the pressure. Maybe you have taken on more than you can handle. Step back and share your frustrations with an objective person. Heightened emotions may be clouding your vision. Take a break and gain perspective.

LOVE READING

In love readings, the Eight of Swords can indicate that you are feelings trapped, smothered, or even controlled. It's time to reclaim your power and stand up for yourself. If you continue to stuff your feelings away in fear of angering another, you will eventually experience a deep resentment towards them, or even worse, yourself. Don't allow people to manipulate you. Remove the blinkers and be honest about what needs to be changed. Create some breathing space so that you can gain clarity.

If you are single, ask yourself if fear is holding you back from opening up to others. History will not repeat itself if you do the inner work and learn to love yourself first.

FINANCIAL READING

From a financial viewpoint, the Eight of Swords can indicate that cash is tied up in something. While it is good to have investments, it is important that you cut your cloth to suit your needs. If you are considering making a big investment (mortgage, car), do your homework first. Now might not be the perfect time to overstretch yourself if you are already worried about making ends meet.

If you cannot see your way out of debt, be frugal and seek professional advice.

SPIRITUALITY READING

Spiritually speaking, the Eight of Swords appears when your inner turmoil is ready to be addressed. Feelings of dissatisfaction let you know that your needs are not being met. Your soul is longing for connection, and that is why you are going through all the feels.

Sometimes, unpleasant emotions arise before we find the courage to change.

Your situation may be karmic; a cycle is ready to be broken. You may not know how to proceed, in which case, seek higher guidance and move slowly. Just make sure you move.

WELL-BEING READING

Well-being related, the Eight of Swords implies that you have lost touch with reality. Your emotions are powerful and all-consuming. Seek the support that you need.

Break free of negative patterns and self-destructive habits. Look at any addictions you may have. Get help with your anxiety. Have fun and learn to loosen up. Nothing destroys your spirit more than ignoring your own needs. It's time to put yourself first.

This card often represents people with mental health issues.

ASSOCIATED KEYPHRASES
Feeling powerless
Stuck in a rut
Immobilised by fear
Ignoring what needs to be done
Worry, anxiety, depression, OCD
Mentally conflicted
Restricted
Not seeing things for what they really are

THE NINE OF SWORDS

GENERAL READING

In general, the Nine of Swords indicates that you have many things on your mind, and your worries have become out of control. Being the insomniac card, it is likely that stress has been impacting your ability to switch off and is disrupting your sleep. You desperately need some rest.

WORK READING

In work circumstances, the Nine of Swords suggests that your reality is becoming a bit of a nightmare. It is important that you have firm boundaries. Don't take your work home; otherwise, your job may start taking over your life. Assert balance. Talk to your supervisor and get some help.

If you are seeking work and this card appears, your job search may take longer than anticipated.

LOVE READING

In love readings, the Nine of Swords shows that you are worried about a relationship, your partner, or the fact that you are single.

If you are in a relationship, you need to clear the air. Don't assume your partner is psychic and knows what you are going through. It's likely that you are feeling lonely or isolated. Don't allow others to oppress you. If you feel trapped, get out. Seek counselling or other means of advice.

If you are single, focus on yourself and how you can regain a sense of well-being. Another person is not the answer to your problems right now.

FINANCIAL READING

From a financial viewpoint, the Nine of Swords denotes worry. Perhaps you are being kept up at night wondering how you will pay the bills. Do learn to switch off. When you are well-rested, you can perform better and put things into perspective. Get practical advice; don't bury your head in the sand.

SPIRITUALITY READING

Spiritually speaking, the Nine of Swords invites you to come home to yourself. For some time now, you have put your own needs on the back burner. You came to Earth to fulfil a destiny, and the time has come for you to align with it. Your dissatisfaction is a wake-up call. Listen to the whispers of your soul and find the peace you are seeking.

WELL-BEING READING

Well-being related, the Nine of Swords depicts burnout and anxiety. You have been worrying relentlessly about something, and it is starting to take its toll. It's time to reach out and share your concerns with healthcare professionals or friends. Let go of any regrets and begin to work through your fears. Take up meditation or the gym. Learn about reframing your thoughts. Create a plan to get you through this challenging time.

ASSOCIATED KEYPHRASES

Insomnia
An overactive mind
Excessive worry
Agitation
Anxiety
Expecting the worst
Sleep deprived
Living a nightmare

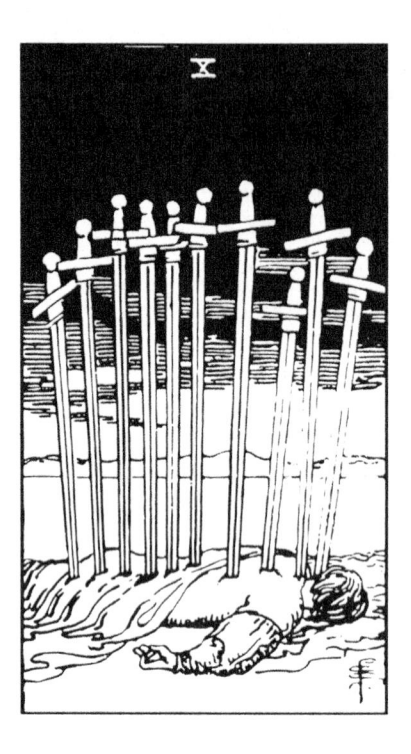

THE TEN OF SWORDS

GENERAL READING

In general, the Ten of Swords reveals that a large amount of mental or emotional suffering has taken place. Recent circumstances have left you feeling totally defeated. A sense of sadness hangs in the air. You have hit rock bottom, and now the only way is up. Trust that you will recover from this.

WORK READING

In work circumstances, the Ten of Swords can indicate that your job is coming to an end. Sometimes, it can indicate that you feel overwhelmed and just want to get out of there. There may well be backbiters and toxic people in the workplace who are making your work life hell. Look for the Queen, King, or Seven of Swords to reinforce this meaning.

If you are unemployed, perhaps this is about to change.

LOVE READING

In love readings, the Ten of Swords indicates divorce or separation. This is a very difficult breakup in which you feel totally floored. There could be a feeling of betrayal accompanying this card. Perhaps you feel stabbed in the back.

Take each day as it comes. Know that what was meant for you will not pass you by. You will recover.

FINANCIAL READING

From a financial viewpoint, the Ten of Swords asks you to be careful with money. Things may not be as stable as they seem. Perhaps someone is trying to pull the wool over your eyes and take advantage of you. (Watch for the Seven of Swords in the same spread.)

This card may indicate that a business is failing, a partnership has ended, or your home may be repossessed (Four of Wands reversed). Tread with caution.

SPIRITUALITY READING

Spiritually speaking, the Ten of Swords is one of the dark night of the soul cards. People who no longer share your values or resonate with your level of authenticity may be removed from your life.

You may be feeling lost right now but know that there is a blessing or lesson that comes with all life's challenges. Notice the person on the card. Although they appear dead, his hand holds the same holy mudra posture as the Hierophant. Something deeply spiritual is at play. Healing, transformation, and growth underpin this card.

WELL-BEING READING

Well-being related, the Ten of Swords denotes feelings of defeat and victimhood. You have been through it as of late. And as a result, you are feeling exhausted and deflated. You need to take great care of yourself at this time. Seek support, fill your cup, and rest.

Do not betray yourself by putting up with disrespectful behaviour from others. If you feel unsupported you may have an achy back.

ASSOCIATED KEYPHRASES

Stabbed in the back
It's over
Things will get better from now on
Starting anew
The end of a cycle
Things can't get any worse
Depression
Feelings of hopelessness

COURT CARDS:
THE SWORDS ARCHETYPES

The following cards represent the archetypal personalities of the court cards in the suit of swords.

The swords or air court cards mainly represent the personalities that the querent is expressing or needs to align with to achieve their goal.

Swords sometimes (not always) represent people with the star signs Gemini, Libra, and Aquarius.

Swords people are intellectual geniuses, logical, and masculine-brained. They can represent surgeons, lawyers, or other professionals. They can be direct and sometimes cold.

These cards often arise when you need to toughen up, be disciplined, act professionally, and be unemotional.

THE PAGE OF SWORDS

GENERAL READING

In general, the Page of Swords is mainly themed around communication and news.

This card often appears when you are about to receive some kind of information that is either unwanted or will be delivered to you without tact, as the page indicates either a child or a childish person. The card also suggests a strong need to ground your energy; this is a time when you can easily get carried away.

Sometimes, court cards are taken as literal people in our lives. If so, this card represents a boy or a girl with masculine-like energy. This child is often very forward; they know their own mind and are not afraid to speak it. They can be sensitive, with feathers that are easily ruffled. This card indicates an intelligent child with a great mind. Perhaps they need a little help in expressing it.

If no child in your life fits the description above, then this card is speaking directly to the inner child within you.

WORK READING

In work circumstances, the Page of Swords can mean you have lots of new ideas! These new theories are in their infancy, so making step-by-step action plans and sticking to them is imperative! Otherwise, your inspiration can dissipate as quickly as it came, and you will be onto the next idea.

Learn to switch off. Don't bring your work home with you, or you may find yourself neglecting other areas of your life. A partner may feel cast aside and eventually become annoyed with your newfound inspiration.

LOVE READING

In love readings, the Page of Swords indicates that children may be causing issues in your romantic life right now. Perhaps they are demanding much of your time, and you are playing the role of the parent non-stop. You may feel as though you are constantly having to solve problems and perhaps you are taking your frustration out on your partner. Let them know what is really bothering you and have a much-needed date night. It will do you wonders.

If a heart-to-heart is required with someone, make sure that this discussion takes place face-to-face. Wires are easily crossed when you communicate by text or email, especially when the Page of Swords has made an appearance. He can be your ally when it comes to voicing your concerns clearly.

If you are single, then put yourself out there! Your curious and witty personality is super attractive. You would be better suited to a more mature person, as you cannot stand immaturity.

FINANCIAL READING

From a financial viewpoint, the Page of Swords can represent money niggles such as bounced direct debits or parking fines. This is nothing major but you will be annoyed with yourself should you get caught out. Be thorough with terms and conditions where required and use your brilliant mind to avoid financial pitfalls in the future. If someone owes you money, be assertive and ask for it back!

SPIRITUALITY READING

Spiritually speaking, the Page of Swords indicates the need to silence that overactive mind.

You are not carving enough time aside to pursue your personal development, which would bring you many benefits. If your inner child has been triggered, make it your business to work through this.

Remember not to take your spirituality too seriously. Have fun and enjoy it.

WELL-BEING READING

Well-being related, the Page of Swords reminds you to balance your time and please ensure you get enough sleep. You may have so many ideas that your head is in a tailspin! There is a sense of hurry with this card, so slow down if you can. There is no need for haste.

Sometimes, this card also indicates that you are being too hard on yourself. The page can represent the little critic on your shoulder that makes you continuously strive and push. Is there an inability to see the value that you bring to the world? Be kind to yourself. You are a wonderful person. Speak and think loving thoughts about yourself.

ASSOCIATED KEYPHRASES
Information that triggers you
News
Act upon inspiration
Don't shoot the messenger
Childish squabbles
A child with lots of energy
Plenty of ideas in raw form
Be in the here and now

THE KNIGHT OF SWORDS

GENERAL READING

In general, the Knight of Swords appears when you feel fired up and ready to go. You are ready for action, but please ensure you are fully aware of what you are about to get into, as you tend to just jump in at the deep end. Actively pursue your goals and passions, but don't allow room for ignorance. Arm yourself with the facts.

If someone is provoking you, it's time to defend yourself! Don't allow people to walk all over you, or you will eventually blow your top.

WORK READING

In work circumstances, the Knight of Swords can represent a clashing of opinions. There may be some opposition around you, or perhaps you have a bee in your bonnet. A person or a situation just doesn't sit right with you. Slow down, but don't back down. Take charge and do what needs to be done. Ambition and logic to get you where you need to be.

If you are seeking work, then put yourself out there!

LOVE READING

In love readings, the Knight of Swords is not a favourable card. At best, it can indicate a whirl-wind romance (see additional cards), someone who sweeps you off your feet. The issue with this knight is he is here one minute and gone the next. He represents the person most likely to "ghost" you in the deck. Don't take it personally; this knight finds it difficult to stick around anywhere too long.

In an established relationship, this card can denote a brewing argument. Tension is in the air and someone is armoured and ready for battle. Take some time out to cool off and gather your thoughts.

FINANCIAL READING

From a financial viewpoint, the Knight of Swords reminds you not to be reckless when it comes to money. Check that you have accounted for all your outgoings before overspending. You've got what it takes to make money, so take on a side hustle and get grafting while you have the motivation and the wit.

SPIRITUALITY READING

Spiritually speaking, the Knight of Swords asks you to consider if you have been shutting yourself off. You have been hurt in the past, but now it's time to dust yourself down and show the world what you came here for.

Don't dim your light. Follow where your true passion lies. Be brave and daring; try new things. Your soul is longing for a little more excitement.

WELL-BEING READING

Well-being related, the Knight of Swords asks you to slow down. You have been so wrapped up with your thoughts that you may be feeling mentally exhausted. Let off some steam and relieve stress with high-intensity exercise. This will boost your endorphins and help you to switch off. Take time to meditate. Your mental health needs to be nurtured at this time.

ASSOCIATED KEYPHRASES
Defending an idea
Taking action
Sticking up for yourself or others
An argumentative person (often male)
Stop fighting
Charge forward
Use your mind
Consider the consequences

QUEEN of SWORDS.

THE QUEEN OF SWORDS

This is the most masculine of all the queens. She is powerful and direct in her communication and magnificent in her logical thinking. She is the oldest queen in the deck, the wise crone.

She has placed her head above the parapet time and time again. Life had wounded her more than you will ever know. Sometimes, she comes across as if she doesn't care or can be perceived as critical. With all her experience and wisdom, she no longer has time for the small stuff.

GENERAL READING

In general, the Queen of Swords represents a cold, steely person (often a woman) who is currently influencing your life, or she asks you to identify the archetype of this queen within yourself. This card demands that you step into your power. Cultivate a keen eye, execute your plans, and confidently deliver your message to the world. You may have been allowing others to take advantage of you, but enough is enough. Set positive boundaries and put people straight.

No one can pull the wool over your eyes; you see beyond the masks that people wear.

WORK READING

In work circumstances, the Queen of Swords can represent a boss or colleague who is proving to be difficult. Perhaps nothing you do is ever good enough for this person. Maybe all they seem to do is criticise your efforts but know that this person takes their job very seriously. Don't take it as a personal attack.

Use the great power of this queen to get ahead in work. You are a fantastic problem solver and a true leader. Just try not to become impatient with those who don't work as fast as you.

LOVE READING

In love readings, the Queen of Swords sometimes represents a divorced, widowed, or single individual.

You are incredibly independent and may not be seeking a relationship right now. Perhaps you prefer to be alone. Or maybe you have been hurt so badly that you choose not to wear your heart on your sleeve. You may be dubious of whether romance exists. Career is more likely your priority.

If you are in a relationship, you may come across as guarded. You are not one to reveal your deeper emotions, and this can cause issues within relationships. People always know where they stand with you, but a little more softness wouldn't go amiss.

FINANCIAL READING

From a financial viewpoint, the Queen of Swords is a great card to draw! Use your brilliant ideas to manifest the career opportunities that you desire. Your keen mind will accurately weigh which investments are worth staking, so trust yourself. This is a good time to look at finances with the long-term vision in mind.

SPIRITUALITY READING

Spiritually speaking, the Queen of Swords reminds you to practically apply the spiritual practices that you have studied so that knowledge becomes wisdom. You have acquired so much information but, on some level, are slightly out of touch with your feminine side. To counteract this, balance logic with intuition. To reach the next level of your ascension journey, explore the interior senses.

WELL-BEING READING

Well-being related, the Queen of Swords can indicate that repressed feelings are now bubbling up to the surface. Perhaps you were hurt so badly in the past that your only option was to numb your emotions to protect yourself. Yet your spirit is resilient, and you have come to realise that avoidance is no longer an option.

You simply must address any conflict within your inner world so that you can make peace with your past and live happier in the present and future.

ASSOCIATED KEYPHRASES
Intelligence
Mental clarity
Quick thinking
Professional
A high achiever
Independent
Confidence
Strong boundaries

THE KING OF SWORDS

GENERAL READING

In general, the King of Swords represents a highly intelligent person. When this card arises, you will immediately know whether it represents an aspect of yourself or someone around you who can help or hinder your situation. This archetype is usually male, a mental philosopher, teacher, or professional who is direct and quick to the point. He frequently appears in readings where there is a dispute and can equally appear as a busy-body neighbour, an undermining colleague, or an emotionally detached partner.

His confident energy helps you to stand up for yourself, speak your truth, and rule with logic. This is not a time to beat around the bush.

WORK READING

In work circumstances, the King of Swords can manifest as a colleague who gives good instruction. If you are struggling, cut to the point and be honest. Someone on your team may seem unapproachable but remember that their goal is to have you working efficiently and at your best. Seek out a mentor. If someone is bossing you about a bit too much, take it up with your manager. Be confident and stand up for yourself.

If you identify as the king in this card, you should be in a leadership role within your workspace. You are efficient, thorough, and have a wonderful sense of clarity.

LOVE READING

In love readings, the King of Swords is not a great card if you want romance!

If you are asking if someone is interested, they are, but they are more likely just to sit back and observe the situation. This person is committed to their own path and will not be swayed from their course of action.

If this king represents your partner, you are offered stability and reliability. Yet, he does tend to come across as cold, distant, or even a grumpy grinch. This person will not give in to their emotions and is much more logical than lovey-dovey. Is stability enough, or do you want more fun and passion? You may be considering cutting ties. Talk it through.

FINANCIAL READING

From a financial viewpoint, the King of Swords represents a person who is very good with money. In terms of income, this king is usually a high earner. Drawing this card suggests you have all the knowledge to generate more income too. A determination to succeed will come easily because you will be fully invested in your subject.

SPIRITUALITY READING

Spiritually speaking, the King of Swords is a wonderful card to draw. It implies that you have come into your spiritual power and are ready to call back all you have lost. Your boundaries are second to none. Ask Archangel Michael, the keeper of your own sword of truth, to prepare your throat chakra to help you express your Divine purpose.

WELL-BEING READING

Well-being related, the King of Swords brings your attention to your head and your heart. You could be feeling void of emotion. Slow down a little and allow yourself to rebalance your energy. You have been stuck in your head lately. You may believe that you must always be positive, so you keep going without taking true stock of your feelings. What conditioning have you been subjected to that has given you this idea that it's good to suppress?

This card can indicate that mental health issues need to be addressed. Equally, it can represent healthcare professionals such as a trip to the dentist or a consultant.

ASSOCIATED KEYPHRASES
Position of authority
Speak your truth
Use rationale
Having a clearly defined goal
A bigger understanding
Law or science
A sharp tongue
Quick thinking

THE SUIT OF PENTACLES

The fourteen cards belonging to the suit of pentacles are governed by the element of earth and are connected to the energies of the north.

These cards refer to situations regarding money, work, study, security, and the physical body.

Earth, in its positive expression, manifests as feeling secure. It is the ability to make and share your wealth. When balanced in Earth energy, you have a deep appreciation of your physical body and are motivated to take good care of yourself. You are not afraid of hard work or study.

Earth, in its negative aspect, manifests as greed, fear, and hoarding. If you have low self-esteem, lack self-worth, or have negative beliefs surrounding money, you will struggle to manifest material security.

To remedy this, place crystals, coins, and round-leafed plants in your home to attract more Earth energy. Spend time in nature and realise you can manifest all that you need, providing that you are open to receiving it.

The angels of the direction of the north are Archeia Ariel and Archangel Raziel. They govern the angels of the Earth. Call in the Earth angels to help you manifest more abundance and attract opportunities for wealth.

THE ACE OF PENTACLES

GENERAL READING

In general, the Ace of Pentacles is a very positive card to draw. All the aces signify good times ahead, and with this card, usually in terms of career or finances. This is a very lucky period and indicates that abundance or money-making opportunities are coming your way.

WORK READING

In work circumstances, the Ace of Pentacles indicates a promising time. If you are already in work, your colleagues admire your strengths and qualities. You are a valuable asset to any workforce. There is so much potential around you at this time. Be sure to embrace all opportunities that come forth. This card brings the potential of a well-earned bonus or pay rise.

If you are self-employed, this card promises great success. You have every right to be confident.

You may have a brilliant business idea in mind. Educate yourself and learn everything you need to know. Adding more strings to your bow will reap future rewards for you. Go for it.

If you have been applying for work, perhaps you are about to get lucky, for this card is perceived as a very good omen.

LOVE READING

In love readings, the Ace of Pentacles indicates a time when you may be investing more of your time in your career/finances than in your relationship. Make sure you spare some of this exciting new energy for your partnership to maintain a good sense of balance. If you make an extra effort within relationships, it will certainly be reciprocated. That way, you have the best of both worlds, thriving in business and relationships.

If you are single, business and finances are more important to you right now. Perhaps this is preventing you from meeting the one.

If your question was about a romantic interest, this is a positive time. Things should get off to a good start.

FINANCIAL READING

From a financial viewpoint, the Ace of Pentacles is the best card you can receive. Perhaps you have accrued some good karma or been practising the law of attraction. Regardless, a welcomed gift will soon be yours for the taking. Good news surrounding money and security is on its way. You will soon be feeling quite flushed.

SPIRITUALITY READING

Spiritually speaking, the Ace of Pentacles signifies that you are extremely well protected right now. Your spirit guides surround you, providing a gentle helping hand of assistance. Those grand ideas you have received may well be their whisperings into your inner ears. Remember to ask, believe, and take action, and surely you will receive.

The Universe is feeling generous. Remember to be grateful for your gifts and many blessings. Share your bounty with others, and your good fortune will multiply.

You may have had a recent epiphany regarding your life purpose. If so, acting upon it will bring you contentment.

WELL-BEING READING

Well-being related, the Ace of Pentacles is asking you to ground your energy. Practice being in the here and now. If you are feeling motivated and in high spirits, make the most of this refreshing period by implementing a new healthcare kick-start.

The energy of the sun is calling you to get outside in nature. Place your bare feet on the ground for rejuvenation.

Any worries (if any) should soon pass.

ASSOCIATED KEYPHRASES
Receiving an inheritance, bonus, or gift
A financial windfall
A good business move
Focusing on money
Good news
A potent time to manifest your wishes
Your needs will be met
New beginnings

THE TWO OF PENTACLES

GENERAL READING

In general, the Two of Pentacles brings you the energy of the juggler. This is an incredibly busy period when tasks and deadlines seem endless. No matter how hard you work, there is still much to consider. On a positive note, you have the energy to get things done and are just about managing. Just don't take your eye off the ball.

WORK READING

In work circumstances, the Two of Pentacles represents a very hard worker. You may have two jobs or a side hustle just to keep things afloat.

You are focused on the game, but is there a way that you could make a passive income? That way, you can take a more balanced approach to life.

LOVE READING

In love readings, the Two of Pentacles can indicate a time when there is an imbalance in your relationship. Work and finances take up too much of your time. Try not to take work home with you. When you are with your partner and family, be fully present with them. This will ensure that what little time you have together is at least quality time.

Perhaps it's time to review your relationship. Maybe you have been keeping busy as a way of avoiding your true feelings. Have an honest conversation with your partner and look to resolve areas of inequality, as this card can indicate one partner making more effort than the other.

If you are single, you are far too busy for a relationship right now.

FINANCIAL READING

From a financial viewpoint, the Two of Pentacles shows you are resourceful with your money. However, you may be at a stage of new growth. To get ahead, you need to invest and are thus juggling finances. Keep up the good work; money won't always be on the move. Before long, you will be building a nice little egg nest for yourself.

If you are in significant debt and can't see your way out, seek professional advice to get out of the rut.

SPIRITUALITY READING

Spiritually speaking, the Two of Pentacles reminds you of the law of polarity. The bigger the wins, the higher the fall. No one is exempt from life's ups and downs. Remember, challenges offer you the contrast to feel blessed when life graces you with ease. Learn to take the rough with the smooth. What is there to learn? Can you find the blessing in the burden? Don't become so busy that you forfeit your spiritual practice.

WELL-BEING READING

Well-being related, the Two of Pentacles can indicate that you are so incredibly busy that you have neglected your health in a bid to keep up. You need to make time for rest and relaxation; otherwise, you risk heading toward exhaustion. It's not selfish to have a break. You will feel refreshed and more able to cope by taking some time out for yourself.

This card can represent someone who is struggling with several health issues. Problems with the ears or their sense of balance may be off.

ASSOCIATED KEYPHRASES
Maintain balance
Multitasking
Busy
Good use of resources
The worst is behind you
Being kept on your toes
Financial difficulties
Life's ups and downs

THE THREE OF PENTACLES

GENERAL READING

In general, the Three of Pentacles is a wonderful and positive card. It makes an appearance when you are feeling creative, enthusiastic, and have big ambitions.

Your dedication and commitment to achieving the highest standards have established you as a valuable expert in your field. Continue to finesse your craft and follow your dreams. Remember to contract staff or collaborate with other experts. You don't have to do it all alone. By pulling together, you've got what it takes to make a huge success.

WORK READING

In work circumstances, the Three of Pentacles indicates that you are enjoying your work. Your exceptional talent is in high demand, and others actively seek your expertise. Your work is immensely fulfilling, making it effortless to pour all your energy into it. Your unwavering dedication is propelling you to a higher level and drawing in additional opportunities, potentially including joining a new team where you can make significant strides.

Remember, do what you do best and allow others to fulfil their area of expertise. Teamwork will allow your grandest vision to come to life.

LOVE READING

In love readings, the Three of Pentacles can indicate that your relationship is essentially solid. You share the load between you, make compromises for each other, and have managed to build good foundations. You have a very practical relationship; you are partners. What you have is authentic.

If you are single and looking for love, this card asks you to work on yourself. You have so much to offer; if you can love and appreciate yourself first, you can build on this when you meet someone. Sometimes, this card can indicate that you will meet someone at work.

FINANCIAL READING

From a financial viewpoint, the Three of Pentacles is a good omen. It signals that your investments are safe and will grow at a steady rate. Sometimes, this card foresees a bonus or an extra sale coming your way. Perhaps you have applied for a loan or grant. Either way, this is a positive time for you financially.

SPIRITUALITY READING

Spiritually speaking, the Three of Pentacles commends you for your commitment to your inner work. Through diligent practice and a quest for internal harmony, you can unify your mind, body, and soul.

Now, it's time to stretch your horizons further by seeking out a spiritual community for support. There is always more to learn on the endless spiral pathway. Open your mind. Be teachable.

WELL-BEING READING

Well-being related, the Three of Pentacles asks you to consider the advice others give you. Seek a second opinion if you are uncertain about your health. Trust your gut instincts.

If you are actively working through a health issue, this card signifies that you have a wonderful healthcare team that understands you and your needs. You will get through this by working together.

ASSOCIATED KEYPHRASES
Teamwork
Creating a beautiful piece of work
Drawing up great plans
Sharing ideas
Brainstorming
Creating security for the future
A shared vision
Persistence

THE FOUR OF PENTACLES

GENERAL READING

In general, the Four of Pentacles talks about money. Financial stability for your future is incredibly important to you. You have been watching the pennies, investing, and enjoying a sense of accomplishment through material gain.

Just watch that your love of money doesn't make you too stingy. Being afraid to share blocks the inflow of abundance. You can easily become trapped in the cycle that there is never enough.

WORK READING

In work circumstances, the Four of Pentacles states that you are very good with money. When you are focused, you have great self-control. This ensures you stay ahead of the game.

You may be placed into a position of authority. You can successfully manage to be in power. You don't let your emotions get in the way of good decision-making.

Your finances and your position are secure.

If you are unemployed, now is the time to think about what you want. Security could be around the corner.

LOVE READING

In love readings, the Four of Pentacles is not the best of cards. It can indicate that a lover (or yourself) is more interested in making money than investing in the relationship. This is where we see workaholics happy to neglect their partners while they climb the career ladder.

It can indicate a selfish or cold lover who seems unable to connect emotionally.

Paired up with the Devil, this card becomes a jealous, controlling lover who won't let anyone get in between you.

If you are wondering how a new date feels about you, this is a gentle heads-up that you may never win this person's love. They are too busy satisfying their own needs.

You may be feeling torn by the head and the heart.

FINANCIAL READING

From a financial viewpoint, the Four of Pentacles is a great card to draw. Your bank balance should be growing nicely, and you should have some level of security. This card may suggest you are quite flushed now. At the very least, you will get what you need.

SPIRITUALITY READING

Spiritually speaking, the Four of Pentacles can indicate that you are feeling blocked. Your five senses may have temporarily lured you from your higher pathway distracting you with earthly pleasures. Don't be hard on yourself – this is probably a spiritual test to redefine your perception of the material world and moderation. A few challenges in these areas allow you to refine your spending habits and self-worth. Remember, it's not selfish to earn a decent living.

WELL-BEING READING

Well-being related, the Four of Pentacles asks you to draw upon your strengths to attain balance. You can be strict with your regime when you need to. Stay committed to maintaining healthy foundations. Don't let addictions get a grip on you.

Healthwise, this card can represent gut issues, constipation, trapped gas or haemorrhoids.

ASSOCIATED KEYPHRASES
Wealth
Security
Financial advice
Gripping onto things
Missing the point
Emotionally blocked
Lack of empathy
Love of money

THE FIVE OF PENTACLES

GENERAL READING

In general, the Five of Pentacles indicates a time when you are fretting over finances. There is a strong feeling of struggle. You may have just lost your job or encountered some kind of upheaval that has resulted in money and security loss.

You may feel alone and unsupported. Maybe you have dependants that rely upon you, which makes your situation feel all the more crippling. You are weary and don't know which way to turn.

Remember, this card very often speaks about our perception. Things are rarely as bad as they seem.

WORK READING

In work circumstances, the Five of Pentacles can sometimes indicate a job loss or a failing business. Your sense of security has been compromised, and you must find a way to restore balance, but the future looks bleak. Do not give up; try to see what works well around you and build on that.

If you seek work, use any spare time effectively while you've still got it. Figure out what type of career you would like to pursue. Then, take action towards making this a reality. Seek a mentor, write up a new C.V., get prepared, and keep your hopes high.

LOVE READING

In love readings, the Five of Pentacles shows there are feelings of discontent within your relationship. Perhaps you have lost that spark. If so, how can you realign and spice things up?

Sometimes, this card indicates that a partner is not considering your emotional needs. Maybe they are acting guarded and keeping things from you. Either way, they leave you feeling "out in the cold."

If you are single and looking for love, become the love that you seek. When you are contented within yourself, you have positive foundations for loving new relationships to enter your life.

FINANCIAL READING

From a financial viewpoint, the Five of Pentacles is a challenging card. Through sheer bad luck or lack of spending control, you have incurred a financial loss that has brought you an incredible sense of worry. This is not a time to take a gamble, lend, or invest. You will not see a return.

Remember the Universe loves gratitude. You might not have what you want right now but make the decision to be thankful for everything you receive. What you focus on increases.

SPIRITUALITY READING

Spiritually speaking, the Five of Pentacles arriving in your spread asks you to shore up some faith. Help is within reach. You just cannot see it.

Your angels and guides want to support you, but if you haven't asked, they will not breach the spiritual law of free will. Learn all about the law of attraction. Use powerful affirmations to shift your ideas about money. Then, tune into gratitude to attract all that you need and more.

WELL-BEING READING

Well-being related, the Five of Pentacles appears when you feel run down. You may be experiencing some minor niggles, aches and pains, or exhaustion. Mentally, you may have insomnia, anxiety, or depression.

No matter how weary you are, please seek help when needed. You do not need to go through this alone. Allow others to help you. Embrace the love and care that is on offer. You will be back on your feet before long.

ASSOCIATED KEYPHRASES

Poverty
Money worries
Financial loss
Unexpected expenditures
Minor health issue
A need for support
Feeling disconnected from people
Imposter syndrome

THE SIX OF PENTACLES

GENERAL READING

In general, the Six of Pentacles is a great card representing increased wealth. There is a sense of harmony within you. You understand your place in the world. The energy of reciprocity is in full flow. Keep the gift of abundance moving steadily into one hand and out of the other.

WORK READING

In work circumstances, the Six of Pentacles reminds you that when you generously share your wisdom and knowledge with your colleagues, you can achieve excellent and productive outcomes. However, it's important to also be open to receiving input from others. While you have a strong sense of independence, your tendency to believe "I can accomplish things faster on my own" can sometimes lead to you taking on more than your fair share of work. However, this may result in a reward or bonus for your dedication has not gone unnoticed.

If your question involves promotions or the success of a job interview, the answer is yes!

LOVE READING

In love readings, the Six of Pentacles asks if you are giving as much as you receive and vice versa. There could be a sense of one partner taking ownership of the housework while the other relaxes and enjoys themselves, or there could be one partner who is more emotionally invested than the other. This positive card suggests you can work through any imbalances and achieve harmony. Keep the balance of appreciation and knowing your worth.

If you are single, there may be more than one choice on the horizon. Don't let wealth cloud your judgement of others.

FINANCIAL READING

From a financial viewpoint, the Six of Pentacles can indicate a windfall coming your way. This is usually a payback of sorts, whether it's a recommendation from a happy customer or, indeed, a simple tax rebate. Good things are coming. You have invested wisely, and now it's pay-out time.

Remember to share your bounty as and where you can.

SPIRITUALITY READING

Spiritually speaking, the Six of Pentacles talks about karma. Your previous actions have led you to this moment, and now something wonderful is on its way to you. Just ensure that you are open to receiving by believing you deserve it.

This card also reminds you that money is simply energy. It is ok for you to be rewarded; in fact, it is essential that the universal flow is maintained.

WELL-BEING READING

Well-being related, the Six of Pentacles asks you to take a harmonious approach to wellness. One day you may find yourself eating well and firing on all cylinders, the next you may be binge eating and over doing it. The key is balance and moderation. See your health from a holistic point of view, and don't get too carried away hyper-focusing on one aspect or anything too extreme.

ASSOCIATED KEYPHRASES
Equal exchange
The ability to give and receive
A financial windfall
Increased support/money
Charity
Generosity
Sharing ideas/resources
Help is coming

THE SEVEN OF PENTACLES

GENERAL READING

In general, the Seven of Pentacles is a promising card. Your hard work has paid off; now it is time to enjoy a well-earned break. You may feel frustrated that your plants have not yet borne fruit. Relax and trust that your seeds are well-planted.

WORK READING

In work circumstances, the Seven of Pentacles can indicate that you are feeling like a change. Your work has become rather mundane, and you are ready to sink your teeth into something a little more challenging. You are well experienced and have an impressive skill set. If you put yourself on the market, something will turn up, maybe not right away, but soon enough.

If you are self-employed, business could be a little slow. Hang on in there; things will get moving again.

LOVE READING

In love readings, the Seven of Pentacles indicates that if you are currently in a relationship, your love is stable. You are strongly committed, and by being fully invested, you can experience the security that you have created. Romance may be blossoming around you.

When single, this card can represent your frustration in finding love. It may feel as though you are getting nowhere. Remember that everything has a season!

If you are attracted to someone, ask them out! They probably won't summon up the confidence to ask you.

Not often, but sometimes, this card can appear when a couple is expecting a baby.

FINANCIAL READING

From a financial viewpoint, the Seven of Pentacles comes up when you have given something your all and are now enduring the pause before the harvest. Don't let your confidence waver. Whatever you have invested in will come back to you. This is an excellent time to make large purchases or invest.

SPIRITUALITY READING

Spiritually speaking, the Seven of Pentacles invites you to reconnect with your spiritual practice. You have been incredibly busy, and the responsibilities of life have been taking over the majority of your time. Slow down and come back to basics. Spend time in nature. Work with essential oils and flower essences to raise your vibration.

WELL-BEING READING

Well-being related, the Seven of Pentacles asks you to wait before charging into the next step of your journey. Explore your inner thoughts and feelings by journaling and deep contemplation. Why have you been working so hard? Have you neglected your self-care to get ahead? Are you keeping yourself busy to avoid facing your feelings?

The opposite aspect of this card manifests when you have been a little bit lazy. Try taking the stairs and get your body moving more.

Sometimes this card can suggest that the receiver needs to eat more fibre. Seek expert advice if your digestion is sluggish.

ASSOCIATED KEYPHRASES
Your seeds are well-planted
Be patient
Your season is coming
Perseverance
Gestation
Hard work pays off
Investments
Long term goals

THE EIGHT OF PENTACLES

GENERAL READING

In general, the Eight of Pentacles appears in a reading when you are immersed in a project or thinking of embarking upon a course of study. Indeed, you may well have already started a training course, and this card is reflecting you as a student. You are hard-working, and your efforts will see you well in the future.

WORK READING

In work circumstances, the Eight of Pentacles says that if you are currently unemployed, take the educational route and lay down the groundwork of your dream career. You do not know enough about your topic just yet, so commit yourself to learning all there is to know about your ideal craft.

If you are employed, your efforts do not go unnoticed. You are incredibly hard-working and have a fine eye for attention to detail.

You are very thorough and quite the perfectionist. You cannot abide by sloppy craftsmanship. You do your work, and you do it well.

Don't be surprised if your boss places you on a training day. You are worthy of the investment.

If you have just completed a training course or university degree, well done you. This achievement will pave the way for your future success.

LOVE READING

In love readings, the Eight of Pentacles reminds you to work on your relationship. It's possible to become so absorbed in your career that you might unintentionally overlook the needs of your partner. It's important to invest time and effort into nurturing your relationship, and the benefits will be mutual. Your relationship is strong but remember to allocate quality time for each other. Life extends beyond just work, and it's important to cherish these moments together.

If you are single, put yourself on the market—just don't be too picky and focus solely on your type. Open up to new possibilities and give different people a chance. You might just be surprised.

FINANCIAL READING

From a financial viewpoint, the Eight of Pentacles is a great card to draw. You have a well-thought-out plan regarding making money. All your hard work is about to pay off. Just keep going now, and you will soon see the returns of your efforts come rolling in.

SPIRITUALITY READING

Spirituality speaking, the Eight of Pentacles connects to your sacral chakra. This energy centre governs your creativity and ability to manifest in the material world. You are drawing in what you need. To keep the flow of abundance coming in, you must keep your inner energies balanced.

Take time to meditate, dream, and utilise the feminine brain to maintain balance, or you may run out of inspiration.

WELL-BEING READING

Well-being related, the Eight of Pentacles can denote that you have somewhat neglected your health due to your busy workload. If your digestion has taken a hit, remember to be mindful when eating. Relaxation and hot baths can help you to release muscular tension.

Remember the saying, "A stitch in time saves nine." Get on top of your well-being now.

Healthwise, this card can sometimes represent sore hands, arthritic fingers or carpal tunnel syndrome.

ASSOCIATED KEYPHRASES
Dedication
Perfecting your craft
Hard-working
Focused
Attending a new training course
Focused on making money
Laying future foundations
Higher education

THE NINE OF PENTACLES

GENERAL READING

In general, the Nine of Pentacles represents success and enjoying the finer things in life. Hard work has certainly paid off, and you are reaping financial rewards. This is your harvest season. Give yourself a pat on the back and enjoy a well-earned break.

WORK READING

In work circumstances, the Nine of Pentacles indicates that your career is flourishing. You are highly regarded in your profession. You are very independent, incredibly focused, and have a knack for being ahead of the trend. You are not afraid to go at things alone.

This card is an especially good omen if you are considering self-employment, as this is one of the key successful self-employment cards. Your idea would be fruitful.

LOVE READING

In love readings, the Nine of Pentacles often represents a single woman looking for love. She seems to have everything except the one thing she believes will make her life complete: a partner.

If you are asking if you will meet someone anytime soon, this card represents being single a while longer.

If you are in a relationship, then remember to enjoy what you have. Try not to control your partner. Draw them in closer by revealing your loving side more often.

FINANCIAL READING

From a financial viewpoint, the Nine of Pentacles indicates that you should be feeling flushed! If not, it's time to assess what you will consider enough, as prosperity is all around you. You are financially independent and do not rely on anyone to provide for you.

You like to have nice things, and you certainly do deserve them. You have earned this time of abundance.

SPIRITUALITY READING

Spiritually speaking, the Nine of Pentacles invites you to live in the moment. If you take time to notice all the gifts surrounding you, a deep appreciation will engulf your heart. Smile at others. Marvel at the world around you. Open your heart to be more generous.

Having people around to share your wealth will bring you contentment that money can't buy.

WELL-BEING READING

Well-being related the Nine of Pentacles reminds you to respect your body by being mindful of what and how you eat. Perhaps a recent holiday or one too many celebration meals has led to overindulgent dining. Or maybe you have been so busy rushing around that you have been grabbing food on-the-go and consuming while under stress. Short-term your body can cope when you eat and drink for pleasure, but now it's time to give your digestive system a break.

ASSOCIATED KEYPHRASES
Luxury
Enjoying the moment
Abundance
Financially secure
Self-employment
Basking in success
Independent
Gain through hard work

THE TEN OF PENTACLES

GENERAL READING

In general, the Ten of Pentacles is always a welcome card to draw. It is exceptionally positive and will uplift any reading. Its arrival indicates that there is much to be celebrated.

Things are good at home, and this leaves you feeling contented. Knowing that your loved ones are protected means everything to you. Relax and enjoy the blessings of wealth and love surrounding your family.

WORK READING

In work circumstances, the Ten of Pentacles can often indicate an upcoming retirement.

If this doesn't apply to you yet, rest assured that you are on the right track to having financial stability when the time comes. The work that you create will have long-lasting success.

If you are unemployed, maybe this is because you are managing a home and raising a family. Whatever the case, there is family or community available to support you.

LOVE READING

In love readings, the Ten of Pentacles indicates that your relationship is strong. What you have is real, and you are both in it for the long term.

If you are yet to settle down and are asking if you will ever find "the one," then take this card as a yes! You will enter a relationship with someone who only has eyes for you. You will live together and have a family should you choose to.

If you are having an affair with a person who has children and are asking if this person will fully commit to you, it's unlikely they will ever leave their family.

FINANCIAL READING

From a financial viewpoint, the Ten of Pentacles represents wealth passed on. This can be a gift, an inheritance, or even by making an income from a family business.

If you are thinking of starting a business, know that you will be so successful in your money-making endeavours that family members will inherit from you. What a wonderful blessing to have surplus abundance to care for those you love.

You could also be thinking about the future, such as making a will or investing in property.

This is a great time to invest, pay off debts, and increase your bank balance.

SPIRITUALITY READING

Spiritually speaking, the Ten of Pentacles ushers in a blissful time. You are feeling truly contented and at peace. The surplus of money and love around you fills your heart with gratitude. Remember to share with those less fortunate.

This card often represents a loved one in the spirit world, such as a father or grandfather figure. It can also be a masculine spirit guide. They offer you strong protection at this time. Feel their love.

WELL-BEING READING

Well-being related the Ten of Pentacles indicates that a family situation may be on your mind. If you have any health-related niggles, consider the fact that this could be the result of ancestral karma. Have you "inherited" your mother's bad back because she used to feel unsupported? Or perhaps your grandfather's poverty mindset because he lived through the depression?

Use physical discomforts or reoccurring patterns as a roadmap for self-discovery and personal growth. It's time to peel back the layers to understand the roots of certain behaviours so that you can create supportive beliefs.

ASSOCIATED KEYPHRASES
Abundance
Inheritance
Family
Protection
Traditions
Security
Family reunions
Retirement

COURT CARDS:
THE PENTACLES ARCHETYPES

The following cards represent the archetypal personalities of the court cards in the suit of pentacles.

Generally, these cards represent people in your life or aspects of yourself. Perhaps the qualities these personalities behold are weak within you, in which case, you are asked to become the archetype to grow and succeed.

Pentacles sometimes (not always) represent those with the star signs of Taurus, Virgo, and Capricorn.

Pentacle people are usually very grounded and well-organised. They are good at making money and building solid foundations.

These cards often arise when you are starting a new business, planning, studying, and investing – basically anything that involves security and finances.

THE PAGE OF PENTACLES

GENERAL READING

In general, the Page of Pentacles usually represents a student or someone learning about making money. It is a very grounded card.

You may have an abundance of new ideas and are excited to put your plans into action. Just don't rush, however. Be open to the fact that you do not know everything just yet. To avoid the common pitfalls, invest more time in understanding the basics of what you are trying to accomplish. Seek a mentor, coach, or training course that can help you consolidate your plans.

WORK READING

In work circumstances, the Page of Pentacles can indicate that you have just started a new job or money-making venture. There is great potential for future success if you can be patient enough with the small wins for now. Success doesn't come overnight. There is still much to learn.

Sometimes, this card represents someone working a part-time job alongside an educational course. Or, indeed, this can be a full-time student.

LOVE READING

In love readings, the Page of Pentacles shows potential. If someone has sparked your interest, this card indicates that a relationship could develop and may move fast. Before you know it, you could be planning for your future.

In relationships, you are a loyal partner and only interested in your special person. You are an attentive lover who knows how to make someone feel cherished.

FINANCIAL READING

From a financial viewpoint, the Page of Pentacles can usher in increased abundance. This may not be a lottery win, but an extra boost to your income will be welcomed. The more you discover about money, the law of attraction, and your trade, the more wealth will come your way.

This is a great time to start new projects and invest.

SPIRITUALITY READING

Spiritually speaking, the Page of Pentacles brings your attention to your home and your body, for they are governed by the element of earth. You may feel called to explore different lands to align with your spiritual calling. Know that you were born exactly where you are meant to be. Get to know the spirit dwellers of your homeland.

This is also a great time to clear out your wardrobes and Feng Shui your home. Out with the old and in with the new!

WELL-BEING READING

Well-being related the Page of Pentacles brings you a surge of fresh energy. You are well-rested and prepared for a new beginning. There is a sense of excitement in the air and this is increasing your happiness, energy and optimism.

Now is the perfect moment to embark on a journey of self-improvement, encompassing your mind, body, and spirit.

ASSOCIATED KEYPHRASES
Study
Learning about money
Small investments
Sowing your seeds
New ideas
Good news
A side hustle
A small amount of extra money

THE KNIGHT OF PENTACLES

GENERAL READING

In general, the Knight of Pentacles represents taking responsibility. He makes an appearance when you fully accept that your actions have led you to this point. You have come to realise that success doesn't come overnight, and consistent hard work is the only way to accomplish your goals. You are contented with your slow-and-steady-wins-the-race approach; it enables you to enjoy the journey.

WORK READING

In work circumstances, the Knight of Pentacles indicates that your career path is steadily building in strength. You have worked hard physically, but you know your efforts are well worth it. Your dreams are invested with a view of long-term success.

You remain relaxed and have confidence in your methodical strategy. Do not deviate from your plans. Keep making headway.

If you are unemployed, your guidance is to get back to the drawing board. You need a plan, or you risk feeling stuck.

LOVE READING

In love readings, the Knight of Pentacles indicates a loyal partner. He can, however, drive you crazy because he can be slow to move and often keeps things to himself. Once you have won this knight's heart, he will not let you go easily.

If you are single, then this card indicates that you will not meet someone in the very near future. Meanwhile, think about what kind of person you might like to meet. Focus on you.

If you are asking how someone feels about you, then it's unlikely that they will be asking you on a date anytime soon. This knight does have you in his thoughts but is taking so much time mulling things over that someone else may catch your eye before he decides how he feels.

FINANCIAL READING

From a financial viewpoint, the Knight of Pentacles is a great card to draw. You know from experience that get-rich schemes do not work, and you have an idea or plan of how you can manifest long-term financial security. You may be in a position where you have temporarily stalled because you need to invest more money so that you can grow. This may make you feel uncomfortable, but remember you have acquired the knowledge you need, turned your soil, and planted your seeds; investments will bear fruit.

You have got this.

SPIRITUALITY READING

Spiritually speaking, the Knight of Pentacles indicates a time when you have a strong desire to get to know yourself. Contemplation, journaling, meditation, and even past life regression will help you unlock the answers you seek. A deeper meaning to life is unfolding. Explore.

WELL-BEING READING

Well-being related, the Knight of Pentacles reflects a desire or need to condition your physical body. Perhaps you have become a little sluggish and are spending too much time indoors. Go outside and allow the healing energies of nature to replenish your soul. Eat better and find an exercise group in a park. This is the time to make your body strong.

ASSOCIATED KEYPHRASES
Reliable
Steady progress
Work hard
Make a solid plan
Do your research
Revisit plans
Commit to your vision
Patience pays off

THE QUEEN OF PENTACLES

GENERAL READING

In general, the Queen of Pentacles represents a time when you are successfully manifesting all that you would like to see in your world. With your tender, loving care and deep gratitude, the Universe is showering you with wealth and love. You are filled with a deep sense of joy and contentment.

WORK READING

In work circumstances, the Queen of Pentacles usually (not always) represents a working parent. Not everyone has children, and this can equally represent someone with responsibilities as a caregiver or with fur babies that they adore.

If you do work, you love your job and are very focused. You give projects your all, and for this, you reap the rewards of abundance and satisfaction.

LOVE READING

In love readings, the Queen of Pentacles is a beautiful card to pull. Your genuinely caring nature has gained you many admirers. People love to be in your presence because, as a natural healer, your energy is very soothing to them.

If you are in a relationship, your love life is likely in a positive state. You recognize the value of your partner and cherish what you have, which is reciprocated. This mutual appreciation forms a strong and beautiful bond between you two. To ensure the lasting strength of your love and continued appreciation, keep on investing in each other.

If you are single and looking for romance, tap into the love already around you. Like a magnet, your focus will attract more love.

FINANCIAL READING

From a financial viewpoint, the Queen of Pentacles is a great omen. You are good at looking after your finances and know how to make money. You appreciate wealth, but you don't let it rule you. You have an amazing ability to balance your work and personal life. This energy keeps the love of what you do alive.

This is a time of great abundance. Your investments will be rewarding.

SPIRITUALITY READING

Spiritually speaking, the Queen of Pentacles teaches us the law of reciprocity. Whatever you give out will come back to you. So, continue to be generous, but do not forget that you must keep the balance by continuing to receive. When you give, do so from the heart. If you give begrudgingly, this indicates your boundaries have been breached, and the cycle of reciprocity is stagnating. People feel good by giving back to you.

Wherever you invest your energy, you will see rewards grow. Remember that everything is energy—even your thoughts.

WELL-BEING READING

Well-being related the Queen of Pentacles draws your awareness to the physical body. Health and well-being are very important to you. You make conscious decisions about what you eat and intentionally take action to maintain good health. You love to exercise and take great pride in your appearance. This appreciation of self makes you a great living example to children, friends, and family.

If this does not sound like you at all, then adopting this queen's qualities of self-improvement would benefit you right now. Make your health a priority.

ASSOCIATED KEYPHRASES
Prosperity
Working towards security
Self-sufficient
A provider
Independence
Nurturing people or projects
Resourceful
A working mother figure

THE KING OF PENTACLES

GENERAL READING

In general, the King of Pentacles sometimes represents a masculine aspect of yourself that you may need to embrace (if you are not already). Often, he signifies a man in your life. This is someone with a sense of authority, such as a head family member, a boss, a businessperson, or a bread-winning partner.

If he represents yourself, he shows up when you are at a stage in your life where you know what you want and are fully committed to manifesting your desires. Through hard work, self-confidence, and maybe some well-calculated risk-taking, you have reached a peak in your game. This is a fruitful time. There is so much wealth around you, and you are not afraid to share it.

WORK READING

In work circumstances, the King of Pentacles is often someone who works for themselves or has a highly respected status in his industry. He has worked incredibly hard and can now slow down and watch his investments grow. This is unlikely, however, as it is not the finer things that motivate this king. It is the ability to provide for his family that drives him.

LOVE READING

In love readings, the King of Pentacles is a great king to have as your partner. He is loyal, dedicated, and generous. He can be a little old-fashioned with his values. He is the kind to open doors for you, and he will never let you put your hand in your purse. He is a true gent.

This king loves nothing more than to spoil those he holds dear to his heart. If this kind of relationship sounds good to you, just make sure your king knows how much you appreciate him. He doesn't need grand gestures, but he does appreciate being taken care of in the small ways.

FINANCIAL READING

From a financial viewpoint, the King of Pentacles is one of the best cards you can draw. It seems you have entered a period where all your hard work has paid off, and you are enjoying a lucky streak. Money comes to you easily and continues to increase. Remember, money doesn't make you happy, but making a difference in the world with your wealth will.

SPIRITUALITY READING

Spiritually speaking, the King of Pentacles is in the flow! People may turn to you for advice or financial support. You are well-experienced in life and have successfully turned your tragedies into triumphs. You have now assumed the role of teacher. Help those who ask. Give what you can. You have so much wisdom to share.

WELL-BEING READING

Well-being related, the King of Pentacles reminds you to schedule time out for yourself. Leisure activities and working out should be high up on your agenda. Your energy output is high, so you must take steps to recharge your batteries each day. You have more responsibilities than the average person, so don't scrimp on sleep, nutrition, and well-being. You feel good now; don't run out of steam.

ASSOCIATED KEYPHRASES
The good life
Financially secure
Successful self-employment
Worldly success
A leader
Commitment
Generous
Father-figure

ALSO BY CLAIRE STONE

The Female Archangels, Reclaim your Power with the Lost Teachings of the Divine Feminine. Hay House, 2020.

Available on Kindle, Audible and paperback.

Meditations with the Female Archangels. Hay House, Amazon, Audible.

ABOUT THE AUTHOR

Claire Stone is a spiritual author and mentor. She is the founder of the award-winning academy The Angel Mystery School (winner Best Spiritual Course). Claire has been exploring her spiritual pathway for over 25 years and is qualified in the following: Master Herbalist, Aromatherapy, Crystal Healing, Reiki, Reflexology, Massage, 2nd Dan Aikido, 1st Dan Mushindo. As well as Tarot, Claire loves bunnies, walking in the woods and making magick with like-minded souls.

To keep in touch please sign up to her monthly free magickal newsletter at www.clairestone.co.uk

Follow Claire on social media

Facebook https://www.facebook.com/clairestone444/

Instagram https://www.instagram.com/clairestoneuk/

Printed in Great Britain
by Amazon